third edition

essay writing for students

a practical guide

john clanchy and brigid ballard

LONGMAN

An imprint of
Addison Wesley Longman

Addison Wesley Longman Australia Pty Limited
95 Coventry Street
South Melbourne 3205 Australia

Offices in Sydney, Brisbane and Perth, and associated companies throughout the world.

Copyright © 1997 Addison Wesley Longman Australia Pty Limited

First published 1981
Second edition 1991
Reprinted 1992, 1994 (twice), 1995, 1996
Third edition 1997

Cover and text designed By Melissa Fraser
Set in Garamond 11/12.5 pt
Printed in Malaysia through Longman Malaysia, CLP

National Library of Australia
Cataloguing-in-Publication data

Clanchy, John
Essay writing for students : a practical guide.

ISBN 0 582 80884 7

1. Report writing. 2. Study skills. I. Ballard, Brigid. II. Title.

378.170281

The
publisher's
policy is to use
**paper manufactured
from sustainable forests**

Contents

Preface

Essay writing for students is a handbook in the craft of essay writing for tertiary students and those in secondary school who plan to continue on to tertiary studies. In it we have tried to explore the very real difficulties students face in writing academic essays. We do not offer prescriptions which ensure success nor tips on how to beat the system. We have written on the assumption, which we ourselves hold strongly, that students genuinely care about their studies, though they do sometimes become frustrated, and eventually disillusioned, if academic courses fail to offer them the intellectual satisfaction and excitement they seek. It is in this spirit that we work with our students at the Australian National University. And it is with this philosophy that we have written this book.

The approaches to essay writing which we have developed in this handbook are based on our own years of experience teaching students the strategies of reading, analysing, thinking and arguing which are appropriate to university study. In our work we are continually faced with the realisation that students do want help in developing their capacities for thinking and writing. They recognise that university essay writing is a different task from writing at school. They recognise that mere rules about format and simplified advice about self-organisation do not help them to grapple with the serious problems of thinking through writing. And they are right. There are no easy answers.

In teaching our own students we always try to work with current problems and genuine materials: the essays they must write, the books they must read, the notes they must take in lectures. We never treat problems and skills in isolation. They are always related to the central task of producing an essay. The approach and methods used in this book reflect our teaching practice. We have used only those materials our students and colleagues have brought to us over the years.

Similarly, the production of an essay is the consistent focus of attention—it is the purpose to which all the activities of reading, thinking, arguing and writing are directed. Finally, we have emphasised continually that there is no one model for developing a successful essay. Successful essays can be very different, depending on the different demands of different disciplines, different courses, different lecturers and different topics. There may be qualities which are common to these essays, but the differences are crucial.

Above all, this book, like the process of writing which it explores, is a dialogue with the reader about the intricacies of a task which has a central role in tertiary education. It could not have been written without the assistance of all those students who, over the years, have participated in our courses or sought our advice about writing and, in particular, those students and staff who have spent time and energy reading and commenting upon successive drafts of this book. We are grateful to them and hope they will feel that their time was well spent.

John Clanchy
Brigid Ballard
Australian National University
Canberra

Acknowledgments

The publishers wish to thank the following for permission to reproduce copyright material: Edward Arnold for extract from *Sociolinguistics* by N. Dittmar; Cambridge University Press, U.K., for extract by A.M. Clarke and G.M. Cooper from *British Journal of Psychology*, Volume 57, 3 & 4; *Australian Author*, for extract from 'Bring back the draft', by Gabrielle Carey, Vol. 29, No. 1, Autumn 1997, p. 23; W.H. Freeman & Co, San Francisco for extract from *Introduction to Contemporary Psychology* by E. Fantino and G.S. Reynolds, and Chatto & Windus for extract from *The Common Pursuit* by F.R. Leavis, 1952; New York Academy of Sciences for extract from 'Discussion Paper: The Evolution of Human Communication: what can primates tell us?' by N. Tanner and A. Zihlman from *Annals of the New York Academy of Sciences*, Vol. 280, 1976; Penguin Books Ltd, for extract from *Introducing Sociology*, second edition by P. Worsley (ed), 1970; The Psychological Corporation © 1955 for figure 'Graph 1, I.Q. by age groups', and Pan Macmillan Australia, for extract from *Triumph of the Nomads* copyright Geoffrey Blainey 1976, 1982.

We also wish to thank the following for extracts used: American Psychological Association for figure 'Graph 2, At what age are we smartest?'; Harcourt Brace Jovanovich for extract from *Psychology: An Introduction*, third edition by Jerome Kagan and Ernest Havemann © 1976 Harcourt Brace Jovanovich.

Introduction

This book is designed to help you develop, in a practical way, your own capacities for essay writing. It will not be of much assistance if you are looking for:

- short cuts or tips or easy solutions to writing problems,
- a formula approach which can be applied to every essay you write,
- advice on how to beat the system.

If you hope to find 'instant answers' in this book, you will be disappointed. However, if you want guidance in the difficult tasks of:

- analysing a topic,
- reading for ideas and information,
- taking notes for an essay,
- developing a structure for your ideas,
- expressing those ideas clearly and fluently,
- editing your essay to meet academic criteria of correctness,

then your concerns coincide with our own.

We have based all our explanations on actual examples and materials drawn from the experience of our own students. The essay topics, the readings, the examples of student writing are all genuine.

How you use this handbook is your own affair. Throughout it we insist that there is no one 'right' way of working through any stage of the process of writing an essay. And there is no 'right' way of using this book. But, as with essay writing, there are ways which are probably more fruitful than others. We suggest that you:

- merely glance through the book first time around, just to get some idea of what is covered. Do this before you decide to buy it; check that it is directed towards at least some of your own concerns.
- use it, or the sections of it relevant to your own problems, when you are *in the process* of writing an essay.
- after you get an essay back, read those sections of the book which relate to points criticised in your essay by your lecturer.

In other words, try to use the advice given in this book in its proper context. Advice received out of context is never much use; handbooks on essay writing seldom make fascinating reading in isolation. But when you are actually in the throes of producing an essay, you may find this book is genuinely useful.

Chapter 1

Clearing the ground

Why write essays?

In the modern world our thinking is largely transmitted by speech and through radio and television—and, most recently, the Internet. At the university, however, you are required to do much of your thinking through writing. In the humanities and social sciences you are inevitably required to produce a considerable number of formal essays. You may also have to respond to multiple-choice or short answer tests, write brief reports or short reviews and criticisms. But most of your more important writing will be in the form of extended essays. It will involve a commitment on your part of time, energy and mental effort. As you will soon find out for yourself, essay writing is hard work—and it doesn't get very much easier as you advance in your studies.

While this may seem a depressing outlook, it is realistic. Certainly you will, with time and experience, become more proficient in such skills as interpreting topics, handling research and sources, and mastering academic language and presentation. But the central intellectual struggle to shape your thoughts into written words and to connect those thoughts into a coherent argument will remain as demanding as it seemed when you were faced with your first essay assignment.

Yet write essays you must. There are usually compelling *external* pressures for their production: they are used to assess your progress; they are an integral part of academic teaching. There are also equally important *personal* reasons for committing your ideas to writing. E.M. Forster once asked: 'How the devil do I know what I think till I see what I've written?', and it is, after all, to develop your thinking in new areas and to new purposes that you have come to university. It is by writing, even more than by speech, that you actually master your material and extend your own understanding. Writing enables you to build ideas systematically one upon another; and to do so over an extended period with opportunities to pause and reflect along the way. Writing is nearly always a struggle; but it can also be immensely satisfying.

False leads and folk tales

One of the hazards you will soon encounter in your efforts to find out what is expected of you in an essay is the misleading advice of fellow students. You will be told blithely, 'Oh, the best way to write an essay is to stay up all night and just toss it off without thinking too much about it'. Another version of this folk tale is that you should just 'rave on', using as much of the jargon and clichés of the subject as you can remember and preferably including material which caters for the known interests of the marker. Such advice is unsound. It may occasionally be possible to write some essays on the basis of a quick response and you may also meet occasional academics who strongly favour certain approaches to a topic. But, as a long-term working rule, essays which will satisfy both your reader and, more importantly, yourself, take a considerable period of thinking, writing, and rewriting. So it would be wise to treat such advice with scepticism.

Another common folk tale is that there is a specific 'skill' or 'knack' involved in writing a successful essay and that if only you can improve your 'technique' or discover this magic 'skill', all will fall into place. Alas, not so. Certainly there are strategies for approaching your topic, strategies for thinking about and researching your material, strategies for the more effective organisation of your argument, and simple skills in the presentation of the final draft. But there is no *one* set of skills which can guarantee success. Just as there is no one perfect essay. And no one perfect answer for any topic. Each essay is, in T.S. Eliot's words, 'a raid on the inarticulate'.

Students are not the only source of well-intended misdirection about writing academic essays. You may find that some of your lecturers and tutors mislead you with superficial comments about the ease of the exercise they have set. They may encourage you by assuring you that 'all you need do is just answer the topic which is set; keep to the point and develop your own clear argument'. How true—but how difficult. You will be told: 'I'll accept any reasonable point of view and any evidence so long as it is logical and sound'. But how are you to recognise 'sound evidence'? And how are you to know what limits the lecturer sets on 'reasonable' in relation to the discipline and to the set topic?

Another common piece of advice is that all you have to do is make sure your essay has 'a beginning, a middle and an end'. This is indisputably good advice; but how to begin, what should come in the middle, and where it should all end, is the real problem.

What then can be done? Where can you start your apprenticeship in academic writing and thinking?

A good place to start might be to find out what your lecturers really expect you to produce in your essay.

General assumptions about your approach to writing

Your lecturers assume that your essay will be a *serious* piece of writing and that it will merit close reading. They assume that you have spent a considerable proportion of time in each stage of the production of your essay: in the reading and research; in selecting and ordering your materials and ideas; in writing and rewriting drafts of the essay; and in the final editing and presentation. It is true that the amount of time you spend on an essay does not in itself ensure success. Especially at the start of your university studies, you may find you are working inefficiently—maybe spending too much time on reading only marginally relevant books; maybe taking inadequate notes so that you have to refer back to the source materials a second time for specific facts and references; maybe rewriting and getting blocked on one section of the essay.

Your lecturers also assume that you will be able to comprehend the necessary sources. You will earn credit not for the mere comprehension of these materials but for the way in which you use them in constructing your argument. It is not sufficient to merely summarise the books and articles you have read, or to string together a series of well chosen quotations and paraphrases from these sources. Nor is it enough to merely describe or narrate what happened during a certain period of history or in a certain novel or play. You are expected to know all this groundwork and then to use this knowledge in order to construct an argument based on the set topic. A common academic comment on an essay which has merely 'covered the ground' is: 'I can see you have read widely and put a lot of effort into your work *but* there is no analysis . . .' or, more bluntly, 'So what?'

Specific expectations about your essay

What makes a 'good' essay? Analysis of comments on students' essays suggests that there are four major areas of performance about which academics hold clear expectations.

In the rest of this chapter we attempt to clarify these four expectations. You will notice that in each case we follow the same pattern: first, we define the expectation; second, we explain what it means in practice; finally, we present a selection of academics' comments relating to it. These comments are taken from a range of student essays.

Relevance to set topic

It is expected that your essay will be clearly focused on the set topic and will deal fully with its central concerns.
In most undergraduate courses the lecturer sets the topics for essay assignments. Whatever the course and whatever the wording of the topic, the lecturer will probably have at least three objectives. He or she wants to develop:

1 your understanding of a general theme, concept or area of material. For example, a political science lecturer will set an essay focused on the nature of 'bureaucracy'.

2 your capacity to handle this general concept for a particular purpose. For example, the political science essay topic may start:

Is it fair to argue that Cabinet Ministers are controlled by their departments?

3 your ability to relate general theory to specific examples.

For example, the full form of the political science assignment:

Is it fair to argue that Cabinet Ministers are controlled by their departments? Discuss in the light of either the British or the Australian experience in the last ten years.

In all essay assignments you are required to read and think your way towards a considered judgement about a complex matter. You may be required to use both original materials (primary sources) and other writers' interpretations of these materials (secondary sources). The first should provide the basis for your thinking. The second may suggest starting points for critical analysis.

In practice you will be expected to:

1 recognise the assumptions and implications underlying the actual wording of the topic and take account of them in the course of your essay.

2 handle the topic and its key terms within the limits of the course and discipline being studied. (This can be a complex matter as it requires you to distinguish clearly between different uses of the same terms. For example, consider the ways in which you would need to interpret the term 'development' in economics and psychology essay topics.)

3 focus consistently on the key ideas and terms throughout your essay.

4 cover all the parts of the set topic. Some topics will include a number of sub-topics or sub-questions related to the main theme.

Lecturers' comments

Good work. You've covered the topic well and put much thought into your essay.

The second major fault in the essay is that far too much of it is not immediately relevant to the topic you chose. The task before you was quite specific and clear. Instead of tackling that task directly and without delay, you discourse at large *around* the topic for page after page. Even your discussion of Y is not made relevant to the central question of X. Why not go directly to your evidence, especially the evidence of the debates themselves (of which you make very limited use), asking yourself 'What does this tell me *in answer to the question before me?*'

I can see that you have done some reading for this essay and understand the broad outlines of the subject, but this is not really a satisfactory essay. It is *much* too general. There are two questions to be answered and they are both very specific. You spend at least half the essay on other matters—such as why wheeled transport developed, or how it was used, or the role of chariots in war, and so on. Much of the first two pages are not even vaguely relevant. This leaves you very little room to discuss the second part of the question. What you must aim for is a tight account of a very limited topic, anchored directly to specific pieces of evidence.

This is a perfectly reasonable essay but, unfortunately, rather off the track. The question asked for a discussion of the role of the *relationship* of X to Y, not of Y per se. There is certainly some overlap and you have, in an implicit way, touched on some of the issues pertinent to the topic, but in all of this you have not really dealt to any satisfactory degree with the X relationship. Did you misread the essay topic?

This essay is all over the place. You start off talking about 'society' as aggregates of human beings, i.e., talking sociologically, and end up using the word to mean something like 'high society' or a collection of aunts in Jane Austen's drawing-room.

Well researched and well presented. At times you wandered a little from the point but your argument was generally quite clear.

Use made of sources

It is expected that your essay will be the result of wide and critical reading.

For most topics on which you are asked to write at university you will find that there is more reading available than you can possibly get through. In secondary school your courses of study were usually based on a core textbook. You knew that if you mastered what was in that textbook you could be confident that you had covered the material of the course. This principle does not hold true at university. Even in those courses for which there is a core text, it is assumed that you will also read widely around the topics set for tutorials and essays. No single book or journal article will cover the material you now need to handle your assignments adequately. (Essays in literary criticism, which often focus on a single text, may be exceptions to this general rule. Therefore you will need to make the reservation 'But that's not necessarily true for literature essays' about some suggestions made in this discussion.)

In many courses you will be given a preliminary list of books and articles. The references and bibliographies in these readings will lead you to further sources—and yet further references. So you must develop the capacity to read selectively and critically.

In practice you will be expected to:

1 read with a questioning mind. Do not accept that something is true simply because it is published or on the Internet. Do not expect that there is any single correct answer to complex questions.

2 read in order to understand both the meaning of each individual sentence and its relationship to the developing structure of the argument.

3 evaluate continuously what you are reading. First, you will need to test the opinions and judgements of the writer against the evidence he or she provides, and against the opinions and judgements of other writers—and maybe against your own experience. Second, you must decide whether this material is relevant to the purposes of your essay.

Lecturers' comments

We are not interested in your opinion but in well founded argument based on wide reading.

Your reading has been nowhere near wide enough. You have merely presented a precis of some of the arguments of a couple of writers. The references you have made to X appear as if they were put in because a handout said you ought to read that if you are doing the topic. Nowhere is there any attempt to present an alternative view . . . Quite simply, this essay is much too superficial to meet the requirements of a university course.

This is a thoughtfully argued essay based on wide reading and imaginative research.

Well done. Based on extensive and intensive research, and giving an independent response.

Much of this essay is simply variations on the same theme. X says this; others agree; therefore it must be correct.

What you say is all very well, but it is only one view. It happens to be the one I share but there is little evidence in this essay that you are aware of the objections which some writers have raised to it, or of some of the problems it raises.

The secondary sources are intended to supplement the primary sources and guide you in your reading. They should be read judiciously and not treated as authoritative. Nobody's opinions (even the lecturer's) are more valid than the sources on which they are based.

I suspect that the main reason why your essay is misdirected is that instead of setting your own objectives and pursuing them by your own examination of relevant evidence, you have allowed your own ideas and objectives to be dictated by the historians you have read. Since their questions are not identical with yours, by following them you were led away from your proper objectives. You have obviously worked hard at reading your secondary sources. The same amount of work put into an analysis of thoroughly relevant primary sources would have paid better dividends. Try to have the confidence to do your own thing in your own way, using secondary sources as critics of your ideas, stimuli to those ideas and sources of information, rather than as guides to (or even substitutes for) the ideas you should have.

A reasoned argument

It is expected that your essay will present a reasoned argument.
In the course of your reading and research for an essay you will collect a substantial amount of material. Facts, ideas, opinions, definitions, quantitative data, quotations, etc.—these become the raw material on which your thinking and your essay are based. They have little significance in themselves. They only assume significance when you use them to develop a systematic point of view or argument.

The term *argument* is used in a special sense in relation to academic essays. It does not mean that you must necessarily 'take sides' or present only one point of view. Rather it means that you explore the topic through a clear and consistent development of ideas, using adequate evidence. So your lecturer will expect your key terms and concepts to be defined, if they are complex, and your general statements to be supported by evidence drawn from relevant sources. He or she will also expect the organisation of your material to be directed towards the conclusion you wish to draw.

In practice you will be expected to:

1 select only points which are directly relevant to your topic and your argument, discarding those which may have *seemed* relevant when your ideas were still developing.

2 structure the material so that the main ideas are presented logically and coherently, i.e. each idea must fit reasonably with that which precedes it and that which follows, and the ideas taken together must lead consistently to your overall conclusion.

3 ensure that each section of your argument is internally consistent, with the evidence, examples, and quotations clearly supporting or extending the central idea being developed.

4 take into account alternative points of view or interpretations of the materials you have used.

Lecturers' comments

You fail to make connections between your descriptive examples and your general points.

You have some real points, but your arrangement of them is disorderly.

Where is the thread on this page—in fact in this essay?

The main problem with this essay is linking the discussion in each section to the main theme. In general the examples you give are relevant to the five points raised by X. However, you cover so many social situations that it is hard to see any consistent thread in each section and impossible to find one in the essay as a whole. You should try to concentrate on a particular issue . . . to focus your theoretical ideas.

This appears to be a mish-mash of facts, assembled for no obvious purpose . . . In effect this is not your work but that of the various authors you have photocopied. You have not developed an argument from the material. In future, organise your thoughts: think what the whole essay title means, and how the relevant facts fit together and in what order, to provide an answer to the problem.

There are some interesting observations here but nowhere do they add up to a case.

In writing your next essay, remember that you are arguing a case. No one is going to be persuaded to accept that case unless it is built solidly on adequate evidence: not on 'reasonable' assertions, assumptions or sugges- tions. Remember too, that you will have a quite specific task to perform; and concentrate your energies on *that* task, resisting all temptations to be drawn aside into byways, however interesting in themselves.

Presentation

It is expected that your essay will be competently presented.
In the final version of the essay you need to pay attention to the formal presentation of your material. There are two levels at which your lecturer expects the presentation to be competent:

1 the surface level of grammar, spelling, handwriting or typing, ref- erencing, and use of quotations, etc.

2 the appropriateness of your writing style to the task.

In practice you will be expected to:

1 adopt a tone and style which are appropriate to academic writing in general and to the special demands of the discipline in which you are working.

2 use the necessary specialist terminology accurately.

3 use the correct format for quotations.

4 follow the form of referencing and bibliographic citation which is standard for the discipline.

5 present graphic and numerical data accurately and economically.

6 edit your essay carefully for errors in grammar, spelling and punctuation, and for precision in choice of words and expression of ideas.

Lecturers' comments

What you say may be reasonable enough but the way in which you say it is simply inadequate. Your essay is full of vague, awkward and misconstructed sentences. I'm afraid that you won't pass this subject until you learn to express yourself more clearly and precisely.

Your expression is sometimes extremely awkward to the extent that the thought you are attempting to convey becomes obscured or mangled.

Stylistically and organisationally, this is much too incoherent to pass. Your problems with expression are serious. Too many of your sentences are grammatical fragments, like quickly jotted notes rather than complete units. And you haven't organised your material effectively. Paragraphs seem to be conglomerations of only vaguely related ideas, not logically unified series of sentences . . . The raw material for a better essay is apparent. But it is unshaped, and the shaping process (i.e. organisation and expression) is an essential aspect of logical and critical thinking.

You tend to use words and ideas rather loosely, without being precise enough about what you mean.

Write in whole sentences, not stock phrases: take care with your spelling and your style of writing.

This is a very impressive piece of *research* and a rather indifferent piece of *reporting*. Your writing is often obscure, clumsy and wordy. I don't feel sure how I should mark this, but on balance I think I should give high marks for what you have discovered and a severe reprimand for your bad language.

For the future, how about using *our* footnoting style?

Bibliography and footnotes are excellent. Apart from a few minor slips, you use scholarly apparatus well and it is gratifying to find a student who gives it careful treatment.

You do at times reach for real insights here, but you do them less than justice. Your expression is very often repetitive, loose and inept. Your sentences could often be shortened without loss of sense, with a gain in precision.

Summary

In this chapter we have attempted to clear away a few misconceptions about ways of writing essays. We have stressed that there is no single set of skills which will guarantee that you write a good essay, but there are specific qualities that your lecturers will be looking for.

The main points to remember are:

1 Your essay should be relevant to the set topic in both content and focus.
2 You should read widely and critically in order to accumulate and select your material.
3 You should present a reasoned argument, based on valid evidence and leading to a clear conclusion.
4 Your lecturer will be looking not only at the material you have selected but, more importantly, at the use you have made of it.
5 You should aim at precision, accuracy, and appropriateness in language, style and format.

Chapter 2

Choosing your essay topic

Having cleared away some of the folk tales and misconceptions about writing university essays, you can now begin the process of producing an essay. It all starts with the list of essay topics handed out by your lecturer. You must now decide which topic you are going to commit yourself to reading, thinking and writing about during the next few days or weeks. Since so much of your energy and interest will be invested in your essay, to say nothing of the assessment value attached to the final product, it is important to choose your topic carefully.

When you first look at the list of set topics you may only be separating those questions which immediately attract you from those which do not. You will probably do this initial sorting on the basis of the *content* of the questions: Do I want to work on *Hamlet* or *The Alchemist?* on ritual or kinship? on licensing systems or the gold standard? But this is only part of the task facing you. This content is governed by the special purpose and emphasis of the essay topic. Are you being asked to use your knowledge of *Hamlet* to explore the nature of dramatic tragedy? or the effectiveness of Hamlet's soliloquies in the development of plot and character? or the role of minor characters in the creation of dramatic tension?

Your lecturers have worded your essay topics with care. They know what ideas and what content they want you to cover in your reading and your thinking about the topic. They may also point out the way in which they expect you to develop your material. This does not mean, however, that there is only one 'right' way of answering the question. What it does mean is that there are limits on the ways you can handle it. Therefore you should, from the very outset, take time to analyse what it is that the lecturer probably wants. This can save you from labouring over an essay only to have it criticised as 'irrelevant' or 'wandering from the point' or 'only answering part of the set question'. This approach will also enable you to read and research more effectively and to take better notes. In this way you start with at least a tentative purpose which you will be able to refine as you find out more about the subject.

Characteristics of academic essays

Most essays in the humanities and social sciences share certain general characteristics. First, you will seldom be asked merely to *explain* or to *describe* a process or event, although this would be a common demand for a school essay. Now the task is more complex. You are nearly always required to combine description with *analysis*. For example, look at this history topic:

> From Cobbett's *Parliamentary History*, Cobbett's *Parliamentary Debates* or Hansard's *Parliamentary Debates*, choose any one debate on any one day (1760–1850) on any issue. Identify the speakers and discuss the issues and attitudes revealed in that particular debate.

Would a summary of the debate satisfy all the demands made in this topic?

Second, you will find that all your essays require you to relate *general* concepts, ideas and theories to *particular* materials or, conversely, to move from specific events and instances to a more general interpretation of their significance. For example, consider these topics:

> Laughter can range from innocent delight to cruel mockery. How would you describe the nature of the comedy in either *Twelfth Night* or *The Alchemist*?

> Can the life of the water buffalo in central Java be described as a clear case of symbiosis between man and animal?

It is the *significant relationship* between the general and the particular which the lecturer is directing you to explore in such topics.

Third, you will find that most essays require you to gather ideas and information from published sources rather than to draw on your own experience. This too may be a contrast to your school essay writing.

Finally, nearly all your essay topics will involve materials which can be interpreted in more than one way; thus there will be a problem or controversy which you must analyse and attempt to resolve. It is unlikely that there will be any one, or only one, 'correct' answer or interpretation. For example, look at this linguistics topic:

> If you had to devise a new artificial language, which could be learnt 'easily', which word classes and which syntactic relations would you consider as absolutely indispensable?

and this philosophy essay:

> Masters or servants. Which are the freer?

Clearly you are not expected to explain definitively the nature of freedom or to develop a total language system. Rather you are being asked to consider various aspects of a problem, select the approach which seems to you most satisfactory, and develop it according to suitable criteria.

Immediate concerns

What do you think about first when choosing an essay topic? Probably content, and what has to be done with it—in other words, the intellectual demands of the topic. Then, there are some practical matters such as when the essay is due, and whether the sources are available.

What is the essay about?

There are a number of different aspects to this question. *First*, you need to check the general area of *content* defined by key words in the topic. Thus,

> To what extent does the Australian environment affect Aboriginal organisation and demography?

is an essay about the Australian environment and about Aborigines, and it is not about Alaska or the Eskimo (though you might, in passing, wish to compare them).

Similarly,

'The poem records a vital change or development of awareness; by the end, he (the poet) has reached a state of mind and/or feeling which subtly differs from that of his opening lines.'

Discuss any two of Donne's poems, explaining why and how far (if at all) you think this true of each.

is a question about the poetry of John Donne, and not another poet, and about the development of states of mental or emotional awareness in two poems, and not about the relation between Donne's poetry and the intellectual movements of his day.

What is the general area of content in this economics essay?

Analyse the causes and effects of a shift in the savings–national income schedule.

Second, you should identify the specific *concepts* on which the topic is focused. The anthropology essay is about the relationship which exists between three concepts: environment (not ritual), social organisation (not economic, though the two may be related) and demography. What concepts can you identify in the Donne essay?

Third, you are asked for *judgement*. In the light of your knowledge and reading, how far can something be said to be true? 'To what extent . . .' implies that there may be at least some truth in the relationship suggested. '. . . why and how far (if at all) you think this true . . .' even allows room for denying the whole basis of the original quotation. It is clear that in each essay there is room for considerable difference in judgement.

Fourth, you should be aware that the essays are 'about' different bodies of knowledge or *disciplines*. The first is 'about' anthropology; the second is 'about' literary criticism. Different disciplines ask different questions. Thus some questions which are relevant and should be asked in anthropology are judged irrelevant to literary criticism. For example, the topic 'Aboriginal folklore' would lead an anthropologist to ask questions about Aboriginal culture and ways of seeing the world. A literary critic would want to consider its quality as a work of art.

Once you have decided what each essay on your list is about, you can pick out those topics which seem interesting. But are they manageable?

What are the practical considerations?

At this stage of choosing your topic many other considerations will begin to flood in upon you. How long must the essay be? When is it due? Does a topic overlap or complement an essay you have already decided to do in another course? Is it advisable to work on closely related topics, or would it seem better to choose something completely different? Is it advisable to try and balance types of essays, e.g., one requiring extensive reading with one involving close interpretation of only one or two sources? Have your tutor, lecturer or friends discussed the advantages or disadvantages of any particular topic? What about the availability of books and other source materials? Does any topic seem more obviously straightforward or more clearly defined and limited than others? Do some require you to start from almost total ignorance, while others can be developed from material already covered? Is one intriguing? or boring? If your lecturer is a specialist in the United States Reconstruction era or in visual perception theory, would it be advisable to select or avoid an essay focused on this area?

There are no certain answers to such questions. They all depend on your own situation, interests and judgement. By considering them, however, you should be able to identify those essays which, for you, seem to be the more manageable. You will then be in a position to choose the topic which both reflects your own interests and can be managed within the limits imposed by time and other commitments.

Making up your own topic

You may, on occasion, be permitted to make up your own essay topic, particularly in later years of your course when you are beginning to write essays involving extensive research. This option, however, brings its own problems. You may find that the major difficulty occurs in actually defining and wording your topic. You should not expect that you will be able to settle on a precise topic immediately. You will need to read extensively and to talk with your tutor or essay supervisor before you can narrow down your general interest in some subject to a specifically manageable focus for an essay. If you do not maintain close contact with your tutor or supervisor during this period, you may find that you have set yourself an 'unanswerable' question or one for which there are inadequate resources available in the library.

Here is the advice one lecturer gave in a handout to students in an Australian history course:

Do not expect at this stage that you can specify your subject in detail. Defining the subject is a process which continues as you work on it and gradually decide exactly what directions you are going to take with it.

Usually you will reduce your original coverage as you move into the chosen field. The research essay is a study in depth which cannot cover too much ground if the results are to be significant. A student could begin, for example, with an interest in the labour movement and federation and finish with an essay on the declared attitudes (not actions) of the Labor Party (not the whole movement) in New South Wales (one colony) expressed in parliament (not elsewhere) to federation, from 1891 to 1900.

This narrowing of focus can be graphically represented as an inverted pyramid. Set out below are four of the many stages a first-year European history student went through in developing a manageable focus for her essay.

Initial general interest

Role of women in French society 1750–1815
Role of working class women in French society 1750–1815
Role of working class women in the French Revolution of 1789
Role of Flora X in representing working class women's interests in the French Revolution of 1789

Ultimate essay topic

Summary

In this chapter we have looked at the processes involved in the selection of an essay topic. We have also touched on some of the initial stages of analysis of topics. (The job of analysis is dealt with, in greater detail, in Chapter 6.)

The important points to remember are:

1 You need to give time and thought to the interpretation and selection of the topic on which you will write.
2 Your topic will almost invariably involve analysis as well as explanation or description and will require you to relate general concepts to particular materials or events.

3 You will be confronted with problems or controversies for which there is no single 'solution' or explanation and asked to make critical judgements amongst competing solutions or explanations.

4 When you are considering what an essay is 'about', you should take into account the area of content defined by your topic, the specific concepts involved, the suggested relationships amongst those concepts and the discipline within which you are working.

5 Your choice of topic will also be partly conditioned by practical considerations of time, availability of sources, and other commitments.

6 If you are creating your own topic, you must consult closely with your tutor or supervisor to ensure that the topic is manageable.

Chapter **3**

Reading for your essay

Let us suppose, then, that you have chosen your essay topic and you are now ready to begin your reading. Where can you start?

Resources: what should you read?

There are at least three starting points: advice from your lecturer or tutor or from other students; your notes from lectures and tutorials; and reading lists provided in the course. Internet (or World Wide Web) sources provide a further, and rather different, dimension to protential reading (see Chapter 5).

Advice from academics and students

Sometimes you may find that your lecturer or tutor is prepared to discuss the essay topic with you at the very outset. He or she may suggest a suitable introductory textbook or a journal article which covers the most recent research in the field. More often, staff prefer to discuss your topic with you *after* you have done some initial reading. By that stage you will be more aware of the crucial issues involved and of the difficulties in finding relevant information.

Other students are often a useful source of information about relevant books. The recommendations of students who have already worked their way through the same or a related essay topic are valuable because they are based on experience.

Notes from lectures and tutorial discussions

Your lectures and tutorials may touch on some issues related to your essay topic. In such cases your notes should provide you with clues about where to begin your reading, and which writers and journals are most authoritative. However, lectures and tutorials will seldom cover the material with the same focus as that required in your essay. So your notes can only be a starting point. In fact lecturers often deliberately set essay topics on content that has not been covered in the formal course. Thus you are expected to develop the material independently through your own reading.

Reading lists

You may be given a general reading list for each course and a specific reading list for each essay. Such lists can provide an excellent starting point for your reading. However, you need to keep two points in mind:

1 It may be neither necessary nor useful to try to read all the suggested materials.

2 You may need to read other books and articles which are not on the list.

How should reading lists be used? Look at the following topic and suggested readings which were given to students in a prehistory course. Even if you know nothing about prehistory, you can recognise how such a list can be used effectively.

Topic: What light do you think can be shed on the early stages of human behaviour by the study of non-human primates?

Reading list:
De Vore, I. (ed.) (1965), *Primate Behaviour*, Holt, Rinehart & Winston (esp. chapters by Goodall & Schaller).

de Waal, F. (1992), 'Intentional deception in primates', *Evolutionary Anthropology*, 1, pp. 86–92.

Goodall, J. (1990), *Through a Window: My Thirty Years with the Chimpanzees of Gombe*, Houghton Mifflin, Boston.

Itani, J. & Suzuki, A. (1967), 'The social unit of chimpanzees', *Primates*, 8, pp. 335–381.

Kortlandt, A. (1972), *New Perspectives on Ape and Human Evolution*, Stichting voor Psychobiologie, Amsterdam.

Napier, J.R. (1971), *The Roots of Mankind*, Allen & Unwin.

Oakley, K.P. (1959), 'Tools makyth man', *Antiquity*, 31, pp. 199–209.

— (1969), 'Man the skilled toolmaker', *Antiquity*, 43, pp. 222–223.

Relethford, J. (1990), *The Human Species: An Introduction to Biological Anthropology*, Mayfield Pub. Co., Mountain View, Calif.

Reynolds, V. (1966), 'Open groups in hominid evolution', *Man*, ns 1, pp. 441–452.

Suzuki, A. (1967), 'An ecological study of chimpanzees in savannah woodland', *Primates*, 10, pp. 335–381.

Wright, R.V.S. (1972), 'Imitative learning of a flaked stone technology—The case of an orangutan', *Mankind*, 8, pp. 296–306.

What can you learn from the reading list?

You can start by linking the list back to the essay topic. What is the content of this essay topic?

- the behaviour of early humans;
- the behaviour of non-human primates.

What might be involved in answering the question?

- a survey of the known behaviour of early humans and of significant studies of non-human primate behaviour;
- a comparison of these surveys in order to evaluate how far the study of non-human primates does throw light on the study of human behaviour;
- your own conclusions on the advantages and limitations of this comparative approach, based on the evidence you have presented.

How does the reading list help to clarify your understanding of the topic?

A quick look at the titles of the books (in italics) and articles (in inverted commas) suggests that there are:

- three fairly general books (Kortlandt, Napier, Relethford);
- two books specifically on primates (De Vore, Goodall);
- four articles on group or social organisation and behaviour among hominids and chimpanzees (de Waal, Itani & Suzuki, Reynolds, Suzuki);
- three articles on toolmaking (Oakley, Wright).

So now you can recognise that there are at least two major areas—social organisation and toolmaking—in which researchers have attempted to compare primate behaviour and early human behaviour. And therefore your essay will probably need to cover at least these two areas.

Which text should you start with?

The earliest? the shortest? or, in a practical world, the first one you find still available on the library shelf? Assuming that you do have some choice, it is probably best to begin with the *most recent general survey* of the topic, unless you know that an earlier book is the standard work in the field. In the prehistory example you would probably start with the Relethford book, which is the most recent book on the list. Also, the chances are good that the bibliography and footnote references in that text will direct you to other relevant readings. (The title of the Kortlandt book *New Perspectives . . .* might catch your eye—but so too should its date of publication.)

Alternatively you may find that a recent journal article would be a better starting point. A book is often the concluding point of an investigation by the writer, and some of the material may well be out of date by the time it reaches print. If your topic focuses on an area of recent controversy or on the understanding of new materials, then journal (including Internet) articles are frequently more useful sources than books. On the other hand, scholarly controversy can be confusing if you are new to a discipline. You can sometimes feel, as you read an article, that you are overhearing a heated argument which started long ago and about which you lack sufficient background to make sense of the current debate.

In any case you will probably begin with a recent general treatment of the topic and then progress to more detailed readings on specific areas. The amount that you read and the extent to which you pursue the details will depend on the demands of your essay assignment. Is it a 2000 word or a 5000 word essay? Are you expected to produce it within three weeks or three months? How much time, energy and interest are you prepared to devote to the task?

If you want to try out your skill in interpreting another essay topic and reading list, turn to Appendix 1.

If there is no reading list provided for your course or topic, then you must fall back on your own capacity to use the library facilities, card or on-line catalogues, accumulative indexes to journals, the World

Wide Web, CD-ROMs, and the advice of library staff. The same principles of selection still apply: start with a recent *general* survey and then extend your reading through the references and bibliographies in the sources you have found useful.

Once you start your reading, however, you will be faced with a new set of problems:

- there is too much to read—'I never have enough time to get through it all.'
- the materials are difficult to understand—'It seems to go in one eye and out the other. I just can't concentrate on it.'
- it is hard to select material from the readings—'How do I know what I'll need for my essay?'

Reading strategies: how should you read?

There are various strategies for reading which, it is claimed, will help you overcome these problems. Three of the most commonly suggested techniques are:

1 Speed reading, which attempts to solve only your first problem—lack of time—but does little to solve the problems of comprehension and selection. This technique is more suited to general reading than to academic study.

2 SQ3R, which is a method developed to increase the reader's power of comprehension. It was designed for school level reading and does little to help you handle the time constraints and need for selective reading at university.

3 Scanning by key words and phrases, which is useful for identifying isolated pieces of information but ignores the need for close attention which is essential in following a complex argument.

One strategy, however, is appropriate to academic reading:

Skimming by paragraphs

This technique makes systematic use of the structure of thought within a passage. In most academic writing the paragraph is an *idea unit*, coherent in itself and also contributing to the logical continuity of the whole argument. Another important feature of good academic writing is *clear signposting* of both the internal connections and the overall development of ideas. These signposts may be individual words and phrases, such as 'However', 'On the other hand' or 'Finally', or key sentences which state the topic being developed. They commonly occur at the start of a paragraph and it is this characteristic of style which makes skimming possible.

By glancing only at the *opening sentence of each paragraph* you can very frequently pick up an understanding of the outline of the argument being presented. Try out this technique yourself on the following chapter from a popular textbook about Australian Aboriginal prehistory—Geoffrey Blainey's *The Triumph of the Nomads*. Before you begin to read the chapter, turn to page 32 for instructions on the steps to be followed.

Chapter Twelve
Trade Routes and Rituals

Trade between distant people is often seen as a mark of a more advanced economic life. If this insight is valid, many groups of aboriginals must have been far from backward because their raw materials and manufactures were traded to people hundreds of miles away. It is probable that every tribe in Australia traded with its neighbours, and a few commodities were involved in such a sequence of transactions that they crossed from the tropical coast almost to the Southern Ocean.

Pearl shell travelled further perhaps than any other item. In Western Australia an explorer saw an aboriginal wearing, as a sporran, pearly oyster-shell which had travelled at least 500 miles from its point of origin. Some of the pearl shells were as wide as a bread-and-butter plate, and their silvery-white surface was engraved with a simple pattern. Many shells were neatly perforated at the top so that they could be worn as a pendant. They could be seen, suspended from the neck of aboriginals, near the Great Australian Bight, which was about one thousand miles overland from their home seabed. Similarly, Kimberley pearl-shells were found as far away as the Mallee scrub lying between Adelaide and the Victorian border. Baler shell from tropical beaches near Cape York were picked up far to the west of Alice Springs and as far away as Leonora (W.A.). Many hands must have fondled those ocean shells in the course of their long journey to the interior. Their journey consisted of many transactions between neighbouring groups, most of which did not even know of the existence of an ocean. If sea shells could travel so far into the interior, it is likely that spears or ochres from the interior were traded in the opposite direction, eventually reaching the hands of people who did not even know that the world held sweeping plains and deserts.

In eastern Australia the axe-stone also moved over a wide area. In a quarry on the smooth slopes of Mount William, about forty miles north of Melbourne, stone axes were intermittently mined and shaped by Billi-Billeri at the time when the first Europeans arrived with their sheep. The stone was volcanic, ranging in colour from black to lightish green, and perhaps was prized in its own hinterland even more than high grade axe-steel was to be prized there a century later. For generations, stone axes from that quarry cut wooden canoes for the rivers flowing south to the Murray, and the axes reached aboriginals as far away as Swan Hill, nearly 200 miles to the north.

A quarry which provided stone fit for stronger, sharper axes was likely to supply trade routes stretching in every direction. As many quarries were worked for generations, yielding thousands of tons of rock, they eventually scarred a considerable expanse of ground. At Melton Mowbray in southern Tasmania the chips and debris of a chert quarry covered about one acre. At Moore Creek, near Tamworth in New South Wales, an outcrop of greywacke running along the crest of a saddle-back ridge was mined prolifically; the axe-stone was quarried by aboriginals for a length of three hundred feet and to a maximum width of twelve feet. On countless still days the noise of the chipping, the patient chipping, must have carried across the slopes.

As the written records were thin in tracing the trade in stone axes from the Tamworth district, other ways of reconstructing the extent of the trade were needed. Petrological analysis was one promising technique. It has been applied as long ago as 1923 to reveal that the so-called bluestone used in building Stonehenge in southern England had been carried all the way from Pembrokeshire in Wales. With this technique in mind an enterprising archaeologist, Isabel McBryde, examined a total of 517 edge-ground axes which had been found over a large part of New South Wales. She mapped the places where each stone axe had originally been collected—old aboriginal camping grounds, trade routes, or simply places where an aboriginal had lost or broken his axe or had bartered it away to a European pioneer. In the laboratory a thin sliver of stone was sawn from each available axe. Each specimen of stone was then ground down to a transparent thinness and examined under the microscope of the geologist, R.A. Binns. Once the minute characteristics of the stone had been identified, the search for its place of origin could be concentrated on those regions or even specific hills or valleys which were known to contain that type of stone. In those areas which had been mapped with intensity the exact quarry which produced some axes could even be located. Binns and McBryde were able to name one quarry which had originally produced the stone for sixty-five of the axes that were found in scattered parts of New South Wales.

This kind of archaeological jigsaw—the exact matching of axe and quarry—can be solved only when every likely source of stone has been discovered and described. In a sparsely-peopled territory the mapping is slow and the geological knowledge is not easily gathered. Nonetheless Binns and McBryde were able to gauge the extent of territory or market which was supplied with stone axes quarried from the long ridge of Moore Creek or from similar rock formations to the north of Tamworth. They found that axes had gone overland through a chain of tribal territories to Cobar, Bourke, Wilcannia, and other points on the plains as remote as 500 miles from the home quarries. The longest of these routes, transposed on to a map of western Europe, was almost equal to a walk overland from the English Channel to the Mediterranean.

II

Stone was probably the heaviest item in overland commerce in Australia. But a lot of the stone was carried in small neat packages. Thus each spearhead from Blue Mud Bay in Arnhem Land was wrapped in bark and about a dozen spearheads were then arranged in a parcel of melaleuca bark, which was as soft as suede to the touch but durable as a wrapping. The bark parcel was then tied with native string. Each parcel was light, perhaps weighing no more than three pounds. In some parts of Australia the rough-shaped stone intended for axes varied in weight but could be as heavy as fourteen pounds. Such stone was tough and needed no packaging. The heaviest stones to be carried a long way were the slabs used as millstones on the inland plains where edible seeds were an essential part of diet but accessible stones for grinding were scarce. The millstones were irregular in shape but their surface was flat. In north-west Queensland some of the sandstone slabs were carried a distance of at least 200 miles to many tribes, and perhaps 300 miles in order to reach the plains along the Middle Diamantina where suitable stone for grinding seeds was scarce. The millstones and the smaller hand-held grinding stones moved in stages as part of a chain of transactions. The burden of carrying them was shared by a slow relay of carriers. To the outback physician who in the 1890s pieced together the pattern of this dying traffic, the carrying of stones across the hot dry country was an impressive feat. 'It seems almost incredible that some of these large slabs should be carried such immense distances: but then, the poor women of course are the beasts of burden.' In some tribes on the plains the young men were the carriers and made long trips with the specific purpose of procuring millstones which they carried home, balanced on their heads like a flat hat.

Much of the ancient Australian trade was in raw materials—in stone, the coloured ochres and clays, shells, fibres and furs, and special timbers used for the making of weapons. The exchange of raw materials was the vital part of commerce, because it provided regions with raw materials which they lacked. Most of the exchanges, however, seem to have been in manufactured goods.

Manufacturing and handcrafts were often the work of specialists, and each locality tended to make certain objects with a skill or flair which was admired in other localities. This specialization was the basis of the trade. Thus in the north-west of Australia a tribe near Cape Leveque often sent softwood spears and the non-returning kind of boomerangs to the peoples in the south, receiving in return spears of hard wood as well as yellow ochre, pipe clay and other items. In central Australia groups living in the west of Alice Springs were recognised for their skill in making the wooden bowls or *pitchi* used as receptacles for liquids. The finest spears were made near Alice Springs, the finest boomerangs to the east and north-east, the best spear-throwers in the south-west, and the best shields—cut from the light softwood of Sturt's bean tree—were made in the north. The scarcity or abundance of particular timbers may help to explain why one region specialised in spears and another in pitchis. Often, however, there was no such correlation. Much of the specialisation had existed for generations, and its origin was even the theme of tribal myths.

In foodstuffs the trade between tribes was not large. No food appears amongst the articles exchanged in the two parts of the Northern Territory—the Daly River and eastern Arnhem Land—in which trade was studied closely by anthropologists. Between some of the islands of Torres Strait, however, yams and other vegetables were traded. There the large canoes provided that cheap transport lacking in every overland route of the mainland. As the root vegetables were not as perishable as meat and fish, nor fragile like eggs and soft fruits, they formed a suitable commodity for trade in those few places linked by big canoes. Above all several islands had gardens and, at times, surpluses of vegetables.

Any trade in meat or fish or perishables required quick com-munications—a rarity in Australia—or a very cold climate. In the cooler parts of Victoria there is evidence that fish and meat were sometimes traded. In the twilight of tribal life, meetings for the exchange of food were periodically arranged near the lakes and timbered hills to the south-west of Port Phillip Bay. Big Buckley, while living with aboriginals on the banks of Lake Modewarre near Geelong, saw a messenger arrive to negotiate one of these meetings. The messenger, on behalf of his tribe, offered to exchange vegetables in return for the large freshwater eels on which Buckley's tribe was feasting. The messenger's arms were striped, and the stripes apparently signified the number of days required for the journey to the bartering place on the upper reaches of the Barwon River.* The invitation was accepted. Eventually the eel-carriers set out, carrying their fish in a wrapping of kangaroo skins. At the chosen site near the river they ceremoniously delivered the eels on long sheets of bark. The other tribe likewise placed their vegetable roots on bark sheets, which two men carried on their head. Some time later, by arrangement, the two tribes met

---

*Buckley recalled that the messengers' stripes signified a journey of fourteen days. It is impossible to see how fourteen days could be spent in a short journey of perhaps fifty miles. It is impossible even to imagine the stench of eels, which by then would have been at least a fortnight old. As Buckley spoke his recollections of this event to a journalist the detail could have been blurred in the transposing. The 'fourteen days' probably referred to the time when the exchange of foodstuffs was to take place.

again at a lake near Colac where roots were exchanged for kangaroo meat. Such meetings were prolonged—often for days after the exchange was over—by the staging of corroborees, by gossip, and by the parading of 'their very elegant, amiable, marriageable daughters.'

These fascinating snatches from the memoirs of the wild white man veil much which we would like to know. Nonetheless they depict a commerce which was very different to that recorded in northern Australia where implements and ornaments rather than food dominated the deals. Moreover, there is a hint, in the trading of the yams and eels, that this was indirectly a way of feeding an unusually large population for a few days on a common site. Here in effect was the biblical pooling of the loaves and fishes.

III

The Australian trade, about which most is known, linked coastal and inland areas in Arnhem Land. Christened the 'Ceremonial Exchange Cycle', it was studied by the anthropologist Donald Thomson not long before flint spearheads were supplanted by transistor radios as prized objects. Thomson had been making a long patrol on foot across Arnhem Land in 1935 in order to investigate tribal fighting which perturbed the government in remote Canberra. Far inland on the wall of a rock shelter, Thomson was surprised to see a drawing of an iron axe of the type imported to the coast by Indonesian fishermen in the nineteenth century. At first he wondered whether iron axes had travelled inland simply as the result of irregular barter. Later he decided that another explanation was needed for the kind of exchanges which were busily made in that part of Arnhem Land.

He found that each area specialised in producing certain goods and in receiving others. Thus a man on the Lower Glyde River, near the Arafura Sea, would receive a different range of goods from each neighbouring region. From the coastal north-east he received a few prized goods of foreign manufacture—calico, blankets, tobacco, tomahawks, glass and knives: many of them he later traded away. From the east he received, amongst other items, black pounding stones which had been quarried in islands near the north-eastern tip of Arnhem Land. From the south-east he received items of possum fur, dilly bags and, above all, the spearheads shaped from stone which was mined in a famous quarry near Blue Mud Bay. Most boomerangs which arrived—for the people of the Glyde River did not make boomerangs or even hunt with them—originated from the south-west, along with hooked spears, ceremonial belts made of human hair, and pieces of wire and iron from cattle stations. And from a fifth direction, from the north-west, came such goods as forehead fillets and heavy fighting clubs.

'Each individual in Arnhem Land', wrote Donald Thomson, 'is the centre of a great ceremonial exchange cycle'. So long as he lived he was under a social obligation to send gifts to partners in remote areas. Generally the individual did not long retain most of the gifts given to him. After a time he sent a gift in a different direction to that by which it had come to him, but always forwarding it to a relative or friend with whom he was firmly linked in the cycle of gifts. Between giver and receiver was a solemn obligation: 'All time, till die, we two people'. Under the power of this social obligation he had to keep on providing gifts for his distant kinsmen: and by giving he gained self esteem just as by slowness in repaying gifts he earned disapproval, perhaps social ostracism, or even illness. He could even die through the combination of his own guilt and the psychological power of sorcery used against him by a disillusioned trading partner.

On the Daly River, about 400 miles to the west, a similar commerce between tribes and within tribes had been observed even earlier by another gifted anthropologist, W.E.H. Stanner. The essence of the transactions, he said, was in the giving. Both males and females took part in the trade and the partners in the transactions were always friends and sometimes relatives. Journeys were not made specifically to exchange goods or repay gifts but the goods changed hands when tribes from the Daly River came together for initiations or communal gatherings during the dry season when travel was unimpeded. In the great assemblies in the open air the goods appeared—the red and yellow ochres, the kaolin, the spears, boomerangs, stone axes and stone knives, dilly bags, the beeswax and resin which served as adhesives, the hair belts, the pubic coverings of pearl-shell and other decorative objects. By the time Stanner saw the exchanges between members of the Mulluk Mulluk and the Madngella, those being two of the scores of tribes near the Daly River, items of European manufacture or design had intruded. Blankets, coloured wool, small tools of iron and steel, and beads and dresses changed hands and were given a valuation which often made the locally-made spear or dilly bag seem a third-rate gift. Even the appearance of these exotic goods, however, could not save the traffic in *merbok* fading as the ties of tribal life fell apart and the traditional weapons and ornaments were depreciated.

There are several puzzles about the exchange of goods in northern Australia. Firstly, was it a traditional trade or was it recently spurred by the Indonesian fishermen who, about two centuries ago, began to come regularly to the coast with gifts of glass and iron? Thomson argued—and his argument can neither be refuted nor reaffirmed—that it was a traditional practice, quickened by the recent intrusion of glamorous goods from the world outside. Secondly, what was the motivation behind the merry-go-round of giving and taking? On this point Thomson sometimes wavered but in most passages of his argument he insisted that the exchange of goods was in aim more social than economic, of more importance as a ceremonial ritual than as a type of trade, and usually more useful in linking remote groups than in apportioning scarce commodities. In that web of relationships, he said, it was more praiseworthy to give than to receive. Stanner agreed, suggesting that to aboriginals the act of giving was more important than the object which was given. So the exchange of goods at the tropical end of the Northern Territory, it seems, was more like a family Christmas tree than a street stall.

Such a sharp distinction between the social and the economic, between ceremonial exchange and economic exchange, is perhaps invalid. The contrast belongs very much to the mid-twentieth century, when specialism was acute and when economists and others believed that the boundaries of economics could clearly be marked with white paint, enabling one activity to be labelled economic and another social. Every exchange of goods is partly social and partly economic. Economics pervade social relationships just as social links pervade economics.

Reading between the lines of the fascinating evidence which Donald Thomson set out in his small red book we begin to see that it was much closer to barter and trade than he realised. The traded articles tended to move from places of plenty to places of scarcity where they had strong utilitarian value. While Thomson stressed that it was more blessed to give than to possess, most of the precious iron axes which had come from Indonesia remained with the people of the coast and did not reach the inland people who craved for them. Both Stanner and Thomson argued that the ceremonial, ritual nature of the exchange could be shown by the way in which the traditional traffic in certain articles continued even when the economic need for them had passed. More conspicuous, however, was the way in which the traditional traffic was re-routed or disrupted by the rise of a strong demand for such utilitarian commodities as pieces of imported glass and iron. While the prestige was said to come more through giving, many aboriginals who received goods did not send something in return. 'Defections', noted Dr Stanner of the Daly River, 'were not uncommon'.

When aboriginal commerce is dissected it no longer appears so different from modern commerce. Dr Stanner for instance argued that the exchanges on the Daly River were not essentially utilitarian because so often they involved gifts 'which can easily be duplicated by the craftsmen any tribe possesses'. If, however, that same argument were applied to the world in the 1970s, large segments of international trade in the hands of big corporations or profit-seeking merchants should also be classified as ceremonial and social rather than economic. A great volume of trade today is in commodities which any craftsmen can duplicate, but the buyers have been persuaded that in some way the item is different: in subtlety of design, in the presence of a supposedly-secret ingredient, or simply because it was made in a workshop or a land which has long had a reputation for excellence. Paris perfume, Scotch whisky, Czechoslovakian glass, Manchester textiles, Swedish cars and scores of hand-made or machine-made products have owed at one time or other a considerable part of their commercial success as exports to social as much as economic considerations. Studies of the tribal trade in northern Australia were valuable but they suffered perhaps because the anthropologists did not realise that the social component which they saw admiringly in primitive exchange was also present in the cities from which they came. In that mistake they were in good company, because most of the influential economic theorists of the 1930s asserted that trade and other 'economic' activities could be understood solely in terms of narrow economic needs.

The exchange of goods in several near-coastal regions of the Northern Territory was not only trade but a vital expression of social solidarity. We can accept the importance of the trading side without in any way minimising the social contact. The economic links and social obligations were inter-twined and it is unnecessary to follow the anthropologists who thought they could stress the social role of the cycle of exchange only by playing down the economic role. The need to trade and to honour relatives could be satisfied simultaneously. Indeed it is difficult to see how else trade could have been carried on in a nomadic society where groups might meet only once a year and therefore had to delay the completion of a transaction exchanging goods. An unwritten contract was necessary for commerce to take place. Credit or trust was necessary when the gift of, say, a spear, was not likely to be repaid with a lump of red ochre until at least a year had elapsed or, if drought intervened, two or three years. The merits of trading mainly with people who are related by marriage or by totemic bonds—in short, with those who seemed most creditworthy—must have been as obvious to a naked man from Blue Mud Bay as to an immaculate man from Wall Street. Seen in this context trade was both a way of distributing useful goods and raw materials and a way of honouring distant relatives by conferring on them goods which were economically useful and productive of prestige to giver and receiver.

The social and economic were lock and key. Without the social bonds the trade would have been difficult to carry out, and the incentive to trade would have been smaller. Without the economic relationships, the social bonds could not have been expressed so satisfactorily nor maintained so firmly.

IV

Not every tribe engaged in trade. Tasmanians, for example, appear to have had little trade. Though the boundaries between tribes appear to have been defined, the tribes sometimes moved far outside their own territory to gather eggs or ochre. Freedom of movement lessened the need for trade. If a group were freely permitted to enter alien territory it could gather the raw materials and carry them home, thus removing the need to acquire those items through formal exchange. Of course the tribe might regularly have had to give presents in order to win permission for such journeys. If this were so, the girls could perhaps be interpreted as part-payment for a trading concession—namely the right to take away raw materials.

In many regions of Australia the economic effects of trade must have been strong. Through trade, some techniques and skills were probably diffused at times, though trade does not necessarily have to be invoked to explain the spread of manufacturing skills. Through trade, many specialised weapons were exported to areas where they enabled animals to be hunted with more success or the expending of less energy. Trade supplied distant tribes with many of the ornaments and cosmetics which gave pleasure and enriched tribal life. But the main economic effect of the exchange of goods was to raise the standard of living in some areas which lacked essential raw materials. The traffic in axe stone and the stone for spearheads was vital to some regions which relied heavily on hunting; without those imports the level of population which the area could support might have been lower. Perhaps more vital was the long-distance traffic in grinding stones to the hot inland plains where seeds provided one quarter to one half of the food in many months of the year. Those plains were mostly covered with soil and sand and lacked accessible stone for grinding, and yet their way of life depended heavily on the grinding of hard seeds into flour. It may not have been previously observed that the importing of grinding stones to the near-desert plains was probably essential for the continued populating of a vast part of central Australia.

Understandably there were limits to the expansion of commerce. Property was for the most part a burden, and so it was foolish to indulge in the accumulation of possessions. Wanderers, moreover, usually moved to the site of the foods and raw materials which they needed, thus lowering the need for trade. Furthermore, trade could progress beyond a certain stage only if transport became cheap; but when that stage was reached with the invention of the wheel, the domesticating of bullocks and horses into beasts of burden, and the building of large watercraft, the nomadic life itself was obviously endangered. For, indisputably, a nomad existence was logical only so long as there was no cheap way of carrying food and raw materials to fixed settlements.

From *Triumph of the Nomads* by Geoffrey Blainey (Pan Macmillian Australia, © Geoffrey Blainey 1975, 1982).

Skimming the chapter

Step 1 Look for *signposts*:

- the *title* of the chapter 'Trade Routes and Rituals' will give you some idea of the content.
- the division into separate *sections* suggests that a number of separate but interrelated topics are covered.

Step 2 Read just the *first section* in full. Read quickly but with enough comprehension to be able to summarise it.

Step 3 Try now to *summarise* briefly the main points made in this section. Your summary will probably cover the following points:

1 Distance over which goods are traded is a mark of advanced economic life.

2 Aboriginals traded certain goods over great distances.

3 Two items which were extensively traded were:
pearl shell,
stone axes.

4 Archaeologists have traced the sources of many stone axes.

Step 4 Now read the following sentences:

Trade between distant people is often seen as a mark of a more advanced economic life.

Pearl shell travelled further perhaps than any other item.

In eastern Australia the axe-stone also moved over a wide area.

A quarry which provided stone fit for stronger, sharper axes was likely to supply trade routes stretching in every direction.

As the written records were thin in tracing the trade in stone axes from the Tamworth district, other ways of reconstructing the extent of the trade were needed.

This kind of archaeological jigsaw—the exact matching of axe and quarry—can be solved only when every likely source of stone has been discovered and described.

In fact these sentences—*the opening sentences of each paragraph* in the section—provide you with a very similar summary of the passage to that which you probably produced yourself after reading the section in full.

Step 5 What can you *conclude* from this exercise?

1 The opening sentences of paragraphs can often provide an outline of the development of ideas in a passage.

2 Intensive reading of the same passage will provide more detail and a fuller understanding of the argument.

Skimming the first sentences can provide you with sufficient grasp of the whole passage to decide whether:

1 it is relevant to your purpose, in which case you must read it more thoroughly;

2 it has little relevance to your needs, in which case you carry on skimming the next section until you do find a relevant passage.

Step 6 Try this strategy once more. Read the *second section* only and summarise briefly as you go. Compare your summary with what follows—again a list of the first sentences of the paragraphs in this section.

Stone was probably the heaviest item in overland commerce in Australia.

Much of the ancient Australian trade was in raw materials—in stone, the coloured ochres and clays, shells, fibres and furs, and special timbers used for making of weapons.

Manufacturing and handcrafts were often the work of specialists, and each locality tended to make certain objects with a skill or flair which was admired in other localities.

In foodstuffs the trade between tribes was not large.

Any trade in meat or fish or perishables required quick communications—a rarity in Australia—or a very cold climate.

These fascinating snatches from the memoirs of the wild white man veil much which we would like to know.

If you want more practice in this technique of skimming, try reading ONLY the first sentences of section III of the Blainey chapter (pp. 28–31) and turn to Appendix 2 to check your grasp of the passage.

Advantages of skimming

Skimming by paragraph units enables you to:

- decide quickly which materials you will read in detail and which can safely be skipped (time and selection problems);
- grasp quickly the focus and development of the writer's argument (comprehension problem).

Skimming is never a substitute for the close reading which some of your materials will require. But it does make it possible for you to read more flexibly and with more purpose.

You may find yourself feeling uneasy when you first start using skimming techniques. You may feel that you are 'cheating' in not reading every word that is on the page, especially if the book is by an authority on the subject. You may also be worried that you will miss some essential idea, and so 'cheat' yourself. However, these fears will be overcome once you recognise that skimming is a skill which you can adjust flexibly to your purposes. The greatest advantage of skimming is that it focuses your attention on the writer's own structuring of material. This puts you in a position to make intelligent choices about what you will read, in what detail, and when.

Skimming for essay writing

When reading for an essay, you are reading with a definite purpose. You are not reading merely for the sake of interest or in the vague hope of coming across useful material. You are reading now in order to begin to find answers, however sketchy, to questions raised by the set topic.

At first these questions may be rather general. Our prehistory topic

> What light do you think can be shed on the early stages of human behaviour by the study of non-human primates?

would raise such initial questions as: what is known about the behaviour of early humans? what is known about the behaviour of primates? what seem to be links between these? and what is the evidence? Once you have begun to clarify your purpose in reading through specific questions, your skimming will become even more effective. And as you understand more about the subject, you will be able to redefine, develop or discard your initial questions. Your purpose in reading will become increasingly clear. At the same time your efficiency in skimming will increase.

If you want to check on the efficiency of skimming for an essay, look at the way you might use it for an essay based on the Blainey chapter.

1 Assume that you have been set the essay topic:

> Discuss the main items traded in Aboriginal Australia and explain the limitations on the traditional trade network.

2 Skim the whole Blainey extract in order to identify the material you think will be relevant to this topic.

3 Think over the following questions:
- How long, approximately, has this taken you?
- You would certainly want to go back and reread some paragraphs in more detail, but would you need to read the whole chapter in equal detail?
- Can you, even now, begin to develop an outline answer to the topic?
- Can you identify areas which you would need to cover in your essay which are not covered in this Blainey chapter?

If you want further practice in using skimming in relation to an essay topic, turn to Appendix 3.

Modifications of the skimming approach

Although you should find this method of skimming genuinely useful for much of your reading, it has some obvious limitations. It may be unsuitable for:

1 the study of *literary texts or primary historical sources* except at the most superficial level, since here the detail, the language and the cumulative effect of the writing are essential to your interpretation of the original.

2 the study of *philosophy*, where the texts are often so densely argued that you need to unravel the reasoning sentence by sentence.

3 certain *styles of writing*, for example, some writers use the first sentence of a paragraph as a *bridge* from the idea developed in the previous paragraph to the idea which is to be developed next. Other writers, especially American authors of textbooks, use an *inductive* presentation in which the key sentence occurs more often at the end of the paragraph and is seen to develop from the preceding detail within the paragraph.

However, in such cases you should not abandon skimming altogether and merely revert to your previous habit of reading slowly and steadily from the first to the final sentence of the text. Even when faced with original texts or philosophical argument you can skim opening sentences and scan for key words or phrases to gain an initial understanding of the structure of the material. You may then want to go back and study the text in more detail.

When the problem seems to lie in the writer's style, rather than in the content of the writing, then you must vary your skimming strategy accordingly.

If you want to see how skimming can be modified to suit the style of a particular writer, turn to Appendix 4.

The structure of the paragraph

Let us return, finally, to the earlier definition of a paragraph in academic writing as an *idea unit*. The whole strategy of skimming is based on the recognition that a writer uses paragraphs as idea units to structure his or her argument and just as there is a structure in the development of an argument in an essay, so there is also a structure *within* a paragraph which is developing a single, central topic. This can be seen in the relationship between the individual sentences within the paragraph. Look at the following paragraph from the Blainey extract and notice the logical ordering of the separate sentences:

There are several puzzles about the exchange of goods in northern Australia. Firstly, was it a traditional trade or was it recently spurred by the Indonesian fishermen who, about two centuries ago, began to come regularly to the coast with gifts of glass and iron? Thomson argued—and his argument can neither be refuted nor reaffirmed—that it was a traditional practice, quickened by the recent intrusion of glamorous goods from the world outside. Secondly, what was the motivation behind the merry-go-round of giving and taking? On this point Thomson sometimes wavered but in most passages of his argument he insisted that the exchange of goods was in aim more social than economic, of more importance as a ceremonial ritual than as a type of trade, and usually more useful in linking remote groups than in apportioning scarce commodities. In that web of relationships, he said, it was more praiseworthy to give than to receive. Stanner agreed, suggesting that to aboriginals the act of giving was more important than the object which was given. So the exchange of goods at the tropical end of the Northern Territory, it seems, was more like a family Christmas tree than a street stall.

Notice how neatly structured this paragraph is:

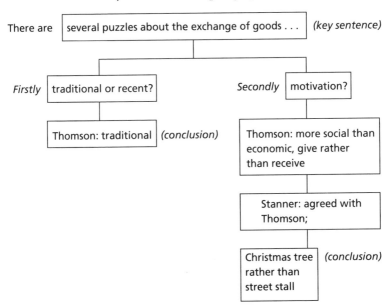

Notice also the importance of the 'signpost' words or phrases in directing you along the track of the argument: 'Firstly . . . Secondly . . . On this point . . . So . . .' These words alert you to the nature of this paragraph: it is surveying a controversial topic, not merely giving you information. In fact it almost breaks into two sections—one dealing with the problem of the age of the trade, and the other with the motivation underlying it.

Had you been writing this yourself, you might have considered writing two separate paragraphs, possibly remembering rules from school days about 'one point only in each paragraph'. However, if you think about it, such a division would have altered the whole intention of the writer: Blainey was using this paragraph as a unit to explore controversies about Aboriginal trade, rather than to emphasise the separate issues of age and motivation.

You will notice that, although academic paragraphs are often long and complex (reflecting the complexities of the ideas being developed), they are very carefully structured and linked. As we have seen, it is this systematic organisation of paragraphs which enables you to skim effectively.

Summary

In this chapter we have examined a variety of strategies for handling the reading which you must cover for an essay. We have suggested that skimming is the most effective skill you can develop for reading academic texts because it makes use of the paragraph as the basic unit underlying the structure of argument.

The main points to remember are:

1 Your lecture and tutorial notes and a reading list provide three useful starting points for your reading.
2 Careful analysis of the reading list will suggest sensible strategies for where and how to begin reading.
3 Skimming is the most effective initial technique for reading for academic purposes.
4 Efficient reading of academic texts depends on your ability to perceive the basic structure of argument which in turn is related to the use of the paragraph as an idea unit.

Chapter

Note-taking for essay writing

Myth and reality

You will find, particularly if you are a first year student, that you are a natural target for dogmatic advice from lecturers, tutors, fellow students and study skills books about note-taking methods. You will also find that there is little agreement among these well-intentioned advisers. Some will advocate the use of small cards to be kept in filing boxes and to be used according to a rigid system for identifying, recording and classifying each point noted. Others will insist that the use of complex systems of numbering and indentation is crucial. Others will express strong views about using different coloured inks, types of underlining, or methods of cross-referencing.

So which advice should you follow? Should you feel ashamed when your history lecturer, in your third year of study, exclaims at your inadequate note-taking skills because you do not use a card index? Or when your geography tutor is appalled that you do not use both Roman and Arabic numerals in numbering your points? Or when your political science tutor is astonished that you're still using pen and paper and not slotting your notes into files on your PC? Or when fellow students who have borrowed your notes complain that they cannot follow them? Or when your own notes bear no resemblance whatsoever to the neat model set out in a study skills book?

In fact, note-taking is a peculiarly personal affair. You are recording information and ideas which *you* have decided suit your purpose. Therefore what you select and how you record it are matters of personal choice. You may pick up a few useful tips from looking at the methods other people use, but ultimately you must develop your own system. And, as you will see, your system must be sufficiently flexible to meet many differing purposes. These will vary with different disciplines, different sources and different tasks. They will also change according to the stage you have reached in your course and in your reading for the essay.

Why do you take notes?

Think for a moment of the role note-taking plays in this long process of writing your essay. Why do you spend time recording material which is already available in printed form? There are both practical and intellectual points you might consider here.

1 Notes are an aid to memory. Obviously if you are reading for a long essay over a period of weeks, or for two or three essays simultaneously, then you must have some system of sorting and recalling information you will need when you finally come to plan and write the essay.

2 Your notes provide the raw material on which your mind must work in relation to your set essay topic. And you will need certain types of information, such as facts, figures and direct quotations, available quickly and accurately.

3 The process of note-taking forces you to:
- summarise ideas and arguments;
- select points relevant to your purposes;
- understand and interpret the original source;
- continually clarify and adjust your perception of your essay topic, in the light of your increasing understanding of the material and arguments presented by others.

So, note-taking is an important stage in developing your understanding of your topic. Your notes will provide the basis for your thinking and the materials for your essay.

When do you take notes?

Again, the answer depends on your own purposes and the stage of reading you have reached:

- In your early stages of reading when you are skimming material of a general nature, you will probably not want to make any notes at all until *after* you have finished your skimming and have got a feel for the subject. Then you may find it useful to go back and make notes on the points or sections within the general survey which seem important to you.
- At a later stage of reading, when you can recognise more clearly the demands of your essay topic, you will probably switch to taking notes *during* reading, or at least at the end of each break in the passage.
- At times you may not want to take notes at all. You may prefer to photocopy a section from a book in order to underline key points or make marginal notes and cross-references to other materials. You will probably want to do this with essential source materials or original texts which you must study in detail and refer to constantly. On the other hand, if you own the book you are reading, then your notes may be extremely brief: mere reminders of key points on specific pages, notes in the margins of the book itself, or even pieces of paper stuck between the pages.

What do you note, and how much?

The content and volume of your notes are governed by three considerations:

1 The **writer's intention** in the passage: The writer has selected and structured the material to meet specific intentions, but these are unlikely to be precisely the same as the focus of your essay topic. Therefore, while recognising the writer's own purpose, you must sift the information and ideas being presented according to your own interests. The same holds true for lectures and tutorials.

2 The **discipline** in which you are working: In disciplines in which you are working with original sources, for example history or literature, you will have to include many direct quotations in your notes. As you will want to include some of these quotations in your essay, you must copy them with absolute accuracy. In other disciplines you will more often summarise passages in your own words.

3 **Your own purposes** in relation to your essay topic: If your purposes are clear, you can select and record relevant material in as much detail as you want. Some students insist that they prefer always to take detailed notes because 'it is all so interesting' or 'it may come in handy later' or 'the book is a standard text and so it is worthwhile spending time on it'. Well, maybe—but in practical terms you seldom have time to note everything you read in equal detail. You will find your notes more useful if they are shaped from the beginning by the demands of your essay topic.

How do you take notes?

So all that advice so confidently given about *how* to record notes is misdirected. Your notes will develop their own format, depending on your purposes and on the nature of the sources.

There are, however, three general principles which apply to all methods of compiling notes:

1 Clear identification: Your notes must be clearly headed with all the bibliographical details you may need later when you want to use these materials in your essay. In practice this means you must record the author, title, place of publication, publisher and edition, and date— or the appropriate parallel format if you are taking notes from sources on the Internet. In the latter case this will include the address of the Internet site and the date on which you accessed it. And next to each key point or direct quotation you must note the exact page reference. (A fuller explanation of procedures, including references to electronic sources of information, is given in Chapter 8 and in Appendix 14.)

2 Flexible system: You should record your notes in such a way that it is easy to rearrange them for the purposes of your essay. Notes made on loose-leaf paper and cards have the advantage that they can be shuffled, combined and reorganised at the planning and writing stages of your essay.

Notes assembled in computer files also have great advantages of flexibility—they can be cut, pasted, swapped, combined and recombined to 'see what they look like together', and scrapped just as easily. They can also, however, be 'lost' (from sight and mind) when not on screen and are hard to look at all at once—an obvious advantage of cards.

3 Room for comment: Wide margins are useful. As you build up your materials you will find you want to add cross-references to other sources. You may also want to include your own comments or reactions to the text, or just indicate that a certain point may be crucial to your essay.

Summary

In this chapter we have dispelled a few of the common myths about fool-proof systems of note-taking. We have also recommended some basic criteria to help you develop your own note-taking methods.

The main points to remember are:

1 The guiding principle of your note-taking should be that the content, style, intensity and format of the notes suit the purpose for which you are taking them.
2 Your notes, whether stored in print or electronic form, should be accurately identified, flexibly recorded and allow space for cross-referencing and comment.

Chapter **5**

Searching
the Web

Research on the Web: some pros and cons

Need information for your assignment? Try the Internet. An entire world is at your fingertips . . . The Internet, however, can be a mixed blessing for academic research. The possibilities and the temptations are virtually infinite. Sooner or later you will need to become a competent navigator and explorer in this new electronic world.

Increasingly, as the scope and usage of the Internet (or the Net) expand, you will be encouraged or even required to make use of its vast resources of information in writing your essays and assignments - along with other multi-media sources of data such as the CD-ROM. You may also find that e-mail and Usenet discussion groups, together with other news and interest groups, have information that is relevant to the field or topic you have to write about. Yet all of these sources, your lecturers will undoubtedly stress, should be seen as complements to, not substitutes for, traditional print sources.

The World Wide Web (WWW), which is easily the most popular and user-friendly way of navigating your way around the Net, may appeal to you as having immediate obvious advantages. The Web can, for example, provide access to:

- recent information (especially recent international information);
- graphical material (photos, art reproductions, maps);
- unusual sources (views and perspectives not necessarily found in standard academic publications).

And it can bring these resources with great ease and speed directly to your computer screen, either at home or in college or in a university computer lab, offering along the way multiple links to related sites. Sounds great, doesn't it?

The more you use the Web, however, the more you'll come to realise that each of these obvious advantages also has a downside. 'Recent' information (whether international or local) is not, for example, necessarily the same thing as 'quality' information. Graphical material can be difficult to transfer or print out, and it sometimes requires special software. 'Unusual' perspectives may be interesting but, if you are fairly new to a subject, you may find it difficult to know whether these views have any worth or authority.

In fact, once you've learned some elementary Net navigation skills, the issue of evaluating the worth or authority of the information and ideas found on the Web can be the single biggest problem you face in using the Net for research. The Web may contain some of the most recent and attractive-looking data, but it is also full of junk. Some of the 'electronic journals' have academic editorial controls and some search engines (like Argus Clearinghouse) provide ratings for various sites. On the whole, however, very little of the careful screening of sources and balancing of diverse views and perspectives that has gone into the setting up of your University library's collection has gone into the accumulation of documents on the Web. There the most up-to-date, scholarly, refereed papers appear alongside high school essays and unattributed propaganda. Anyone with a minimum of technical expertise can put anything on the Web (given the normal restrictions on pornography and violence)—and they do.

How, then, can you decide what items of information from the Web sites you visit are likely to be authoritative enough to use in support of an argument in your essay or assignment?

Evaluating information from the WWW

First of all, some of the criteria you use for evaluating information from the Web are the same as the criteria you would use for selecting information from books and journals—criteria which we have already talked about earlier in this book. You may just need to be more cautious in assessing the Net materials.

For example, you will need to be clear and confident about your *purpose* in searching the Web in the first place. In this context, as we have seen in previous chapters, your purpose is set by the terms of your essay topic. It is this purpose that shapes the way you search for sources, the way you read and when you make notes, regardless of whether you're working with printed materials or from a computer screen. Yet it is the nature of the Web itself that can cause you headaches. The Web is precisely what its name suggests—a web: an intricate, highly sophisticated, interconnected collection of sites through which you can wander almost endlessly via in-built links. These links can lead you out along tempting sidetracks but, if you are not mindful of your controlling purpose, you may finish two weeks research with pages and pages of 'amazing' references and only the haziest idea of your original topic and line of argument—and no time to sort it all out and get your essay actually written.

As well as this overriding importance of the *purpose* of your search for information, what other common criteria apply to both printed and electronic sources? Here are four you may need to think about:

• **relevance**	• Which questions or issues in my essay topic does this material specifically relate to?
• **comprehensiveness & balance**	• Does the material I've found present a complete or only partial account of the topic?
	• Is it written from a particular perspective or with a particular 'interest' in mind? Does it take account of other perspectives? Is there obvious bias?
	• Does it display a familiarity with theories, concepts and methods I've become used to in this subject area?
• **persuasiveness**	• Is the material clearly structured?
	• Does it follow a consistent approach or line of argument?
	• Does it provide evidence for its claims? How good is the evidence?
• **competence**	• Do the data in the material appear to be accurate?
	• Does the author provide ways of checking data and claims (e.g. textual references, a bibliography, links to other sources)?
	• Is specialist terminology used correctly? Is the material generally well written?

These common criteria may sound familiar to you. In fact they correspond very closely to the four criteria we set out in Chapter 1 for your own essays (your essay should be relevant; it should be the result of wide and critical reading; it should present a reasoned argument; and it should be competently presented). In other words, the criteria *you* should use in evaluating potential material for your essay correspond closely with the criteria *your lecturer* will use in evaluating your written assignment.

Special criteria for the Web

In addition to these common criteria, there are two other special considerations in evaluating material you find on the Web. The first relates to the **author** (and **publisher**) of the material, and the second to its **currency**. These are of particular importance because of the potential anonymity of the WWW and the fragility and instability of the sites within it. In other words, not only can the identity and status of a Web author remain unknown, but the material he or she places on it can appear—and disappear—with disconcerting speed. This creates special problems if you want to use Web material in your essays (particularly if you can't find the same or similar data elsewhere): you may not be able to find the material again even a week later, and your lecturers will have the same problem if they want to check on your sources.

So, there are some additional questions you need to keep in mind about information you get from the Web. First, there is the matter of **authorship**.

• **author & publisher**	• Is the author of the material clearly identified? By name? By title and professional status? Is the author of the document you are accessing the same person as the original creator of the material?
	• Is the author well-known in your subject field? Is he or she referred to in any other documents or by any other author whom you trust or whom your lecturer has recommended?
	• If the document is associated with or published by an institution, is the publisher (the server) identified? If so, is it an institution with some claim to authority (e.g. a university department, research institute, discipline journal, major newspaper or publisher)?

A knowledge of authorship and publication can be crucial in deciding how you interpret and what weight you give to documents on the Web. If you are a student of Asian studies, for example, and you are searching the Web for an essay on the politics of modern Burma, you will find a great deal of current material—a lot of it with seemingly insider knowledge—on the WWW. What difference would it make to your use and interpretation of such material, however, if you found out that the largest portion of it was produced by the agents of SLORC (the military government ruling Burma) and, on the other side, the next largest portion was produced by dissident Burmese students and overseas anti-SLORC pressure groups? You might still want to use such information, but you might need to treat the views it expresses more cautiously than, say, material you found in the proceedings of a conference on recent developments in Burma published (whether electronically or in print) by an academic department of a University.

The second question you need to take into account in evaluating Web documents is **currency**. The following questions may give you some guidance in how to assess this matter.

• **currency**	• Is it clear when the document was created?
	• When was it revised (Does the bottom of the Web page have a 'last updated' date? Does the directory in which the document resides have a 'last modified' date?) Is there evidence of its being frequently revised?
	• Are the data in the document relatively recent? (Look for internal confirmation, e.g. what dates are given for tables or statistical information or quotes, either in the document or in its bibliography?)

The date at which material is posted on the Web, like the date on a newspaper, gives both you and your reader a sense of how that evidence is to be evaluated.

Of course there are other aesthetic or technical criteria you can apply in evaluating WWW materials: how well laid out is the information? how useful and comprehensive are the links? how easy is it to make your way around the site? and—using any out-links—how easy is to move from site to site, and back again? are the graphics functional or merely decorative? etc. But these criteria regarding the *form* of the Web documents you are using are secondary to our concern here with the *intellectual worth* of those documents. Certainly form is important. A document that is sloppily presented and that shows no obvious attention to details of format may go hand in hand with poor scholarship—on a Web site just as in an essay. On the other hand, the most meticulous attention to format will not, of itself, guarantee that a Web document is anything more than 'just another load of old cyberjunk'.

You'll need to go through similar processes to evaluate information you get from e-mail, news and discussion groups, and other interactive sources. The information itself may, in your judgement, be highly relevant to your topic, but it can only be given the same limited status as a personal comment from an individual or a discussion in a tutorial— and it should be similarly referenced (see *Appendices 14 and 15*).

If you are interested in following up either the intellectual or the technical issues touched on in this chapter, you will find a number of useful documents—most of them produced by American academics— on the Web itself. Start your search by using keywords such as 'Internet' (or 'World Wide Web') in conjunction with 'Evaluating Resources' or 'Evaluating Information' or 'Thinking Critically' or 'Quality'—and when you find such a site, put theory into practice and evaluate the site itself against the two criteria of *author* (*and publisher*) and *currency* listed above. (Failing that, you can refer to a regularly updated printed guide such as *The Internet: The Rough Guide*. See *Appendix 12* for details of this and other useful printed texts in the area of electronic research and publication.)

So, happy surfing. But keep one eye out for rocks . . .

Summary

In this chapter we have addressed some of the issues and questions you should keep in mind when you search the World Wide Web for information for your essays and assignments. We have stressed that while some documents on the Web are very carefully screened and evaluated, many others are not given any prior critical appraisal at all. The Web is thus both a goldmine and a junkyard.

The main points to remember are:

1 The bulk of material on the Web is poorly organised and is not selected or validated by any authority. You will need, therefore, to maintain a clear sense of your purpose in accessing Web material in the first place and a highly critical attitude to its interpretation and use.
2 Some of the criteria by which you evaluate Web documents are very similar to those you bring to print sources, in particular: relevance, comprehensiveness and balance, persuasiveness, and competence.
3 In addition, for Web documents issues of authorship (and publication) and currency assume particular importance.

Chapter **6**

Analysing and planning

Sooner or later you will arrive at the point when you need to switch from gathering material to planning how you will develop it into an essay. How will you decide when this critical point is reached? Isn't there time to read 'just one more book'? Or 'to wait for another week in case the topic is covered in a lecture'? You may feel very hesitant about actually committing your ideas to paper. Yet the more experienced you become as a student, the more clearly you will realise the danger of postponing the plunge into planning and writing.

In practice, you'll probably get started because you have to—because the deadline is dangerously close.

So what is the next step you must take?

Analysing your essay topic

You may find it useful to begin by going back to the essay topic—not to look for clues about content but to analyse the ways in which you are being directed to use this material. What exactly is it that you are being asked to do with it all?

Look first for the key words which direct *how* the content is to be handled. For example, which are the key directional words in this prehistory topic?

Describe the hominid remains from the Koobi Fora sites. How do they compare with remains from other early African sites?

The first part of the topic seems to be straightforward. You are asked to *describe* prehistoric remains from a specific location. The terms in which you describe the remains and the characteristics you select for description (number? size? colour? shape? placement? etc.) would be those you were taught to use in the prehistory course.

The second demand made in this topic is more complex.

The directional word *compare* involves much more than mere description. It requires some form of *analysis*. For what purpose are you being asked to 'compare' two or more sets of hominid remains? Presumably to discover similarities and differences. And then to draw some general conclusions about what is significant in these points. Notice that the wording of the topic does not explicitly state that you must draw conclusions—but you will always be expected to do so. In other words, you are comparing the hominid remains in order to establish origins, causes and relationships. As soon as you begin to point to similarities and draw conclusions from them (for example, 'The remains at Koobi Fora and at X are so similar as to suggest that these hominids were derived from common ancestral stock . . .'), you are in the process of analysing your material.

The tasks of *describing* and *analysing* are common requirements in university essay topics. The task of describing may be identified by directional words such as 'explain', 'review', 'outline', 'enumerate', 'list', 'summarise', 'state'. Words which direct you to analyse your material include 'assess', 'compare', 'contrast', 'criticise', 'analyse', 'discuss'.

Look carefully now at these three essay topics. Can you recognise the point at which you are being asked to shift from describing your material to analysing it?

The science of psychology is based on verifiable data. Experimentation is only one way such data is collected. Other methods include observation, surveys, tests, and case histories. Select one method and describe it at length, noting its advantages and disadvantages. (*psychology*)

List three methods of absolute dating and three of relative dating. For one of the absolute methods, describe how it is carried out, its application and its limitations. (*geography*)

What is a 'phoneme'? What is a 'morpheme'? Compare and contrast the status and function of the phoneme as the central unit of phonology, and the morpheme as the central unit of morphology. (*linguistics*)

In addition to description and analysis, university essay topics commonly contain three other types of tasks:

- evaluation of controversy,
- definition or clarification,
- interpretation.

Evaluation of controversy

Look at the following topic from political science:

'Ministers provide a convenient facade for bureaucratic rule.' Do you agree?

This quotation contains a very strong value judgement. You can assume that it has been deliberately chosen or created for its provocative potential. This form of topic is very common: a strongly biased or controversial view of a complex issue is expressed and you are simply directed to 'discuss' it or asked 'do you agree?'. (The latter, of course, always includes the unexpressed 'or do you disagree?' and 'why?'.) This is a task of *evaluation*.

What are you being asked to 'evaluate' in this topic? The view that 'ministers provide a convenient facade'? 'Convenient' for whom? the ministers or the bureaucrats? or both? 'Convenient' in what way? Ministers can always blame public servants for bungles? Ministers are left by public servants with responsibility for errors? What is a 'facade'? a front? necessarily a *false* front? (Better check this in a dictionary . . .)

When dealing with a controversial statement, start by 'arguing' with it. Raise questions. Try to dig down to the implications and values underlying the wording of the topic. Get your mind moving on the issues. You will usually find you don't want to agree or disagree totally with a deliberately biased statement. In the political science question 'Do you agree?' not only includes 'or do you disagree?' and 'why?' but also '*to what extent* do you agree or disagree?' Totally? in part? with one, two, three reservations? with some minor objections?

Words and phrases which explicitly indicate the need for evaluation include 'to what extent', 'in what ways', 'how far', 'how valid', 'assess'. However, in some topics the demand for evaluation is only implicit. For example, if you were asked in psychology to:

Review the factors (biological, environmental, and measurement) that are the primary sources of variation in IQ scores . . .

you would find, on the most superficial reading of the literature, that the biological source of variation in IQ scores is a highly controversial matter. Some authorities hold that it is the most significant factor of influence; others that it is the least. You will then realise that in order to 'review the factors' you must necessarily evaluate the conflicting views and evidence.

Look now at these topics and see if you can recognise what you are being asked to evaluate.

'Permitting unrestricted imports of goods produced by cheap labour is just like having migrants enter the country and take jobs away from citizens.' Assess this statement. (*economics*)

Compare and contrast theories of learned versus innate aggression. (*psychology*)

'Donne's poetry is disagreeably self-centred.' Discuss any two of his poems, explaining how far you think this true of each (if not, why not) and how in each case this affects your judgement of the poem's merit. (*English*)

'The poor health of most Aborigines is due more to cultural factors than to the inadequate provision of health services.' Do you agree? (*anthropology*)

Definition or clarification

You will find that in most topics you have to clarify or define key terms or concepts before you can get down to the central task of the essay. However in some essays the central task is one of definition and clarification. For example, this philosophy topic:

How do we know whether other people are happy? Can we know, beyond the possibility of illusion, whether we ourselves are happy?

Clearly these questions are directing you to define what we mean by saying 'people are happy', and what we mean by saying 'we know' something to be true. Equally clearly, simple dictionary definitions will not do. The whole task involves you in the process of gradually clarifying the nature of 'happiness' and the grounds on which 'knowing' rests. (If by 'happy' we mean X, then . . . but if we mean Y, then . . .) This process of definition is itself the answer to the questions you have been set.

Similarly, the following history topic:

Was there a 'revolution' in North America between c. 1763 and 1800?

centres on the appropriateness of the term 'revolution' as a definition of certain events (revolution? evolution? rebellion? revolt? resistance?). This can be judged only in terms of your understanding of the events as presented in primary documents and other sources.

The following topics also involve tasks of definition. Which terms are you being asked to clarify in each question?

Is *Scarlet and Black* a story of success or failure? (*European literature and society*)

'Tools Makyth Man.' In the light of the present archaeological evidence what do you think can be said in support or criticism of this definition? (*prehistory*)

Is the Presidency a 'democratic' institution? (*American history*)

Interpretation

Interpretation is closely related to translation. Literary criticism, for example, is largely an act of interpretation in which you explore the meaning and values created in a literary work in terms other than those of the work itself. Here is an exercise in practical criticism:

Write an account of Ted Hughes' poem 'Wind' which will consider, among other things, the central concern; the author's vocabulary; his use of imagery. Do you find his vocabulary and imagery appropriate, or artificial and overstrained, or original and stimulating? Are there any passages you would single out for praise or blame? For what reasons?

This exercise involves a certain amount of paraphrase (a restatement in your own words of the poem's meaning), critical comment upon the vocabulary and imagery of the poem, and judgement of the degree to which the poem is successful. All of these—paraphrase, critical comment, judgement—are part of the act of literary interpretation.

The task of interpretation may also be central to other disciplines. In history and prehistory, for example, you may be asked to interpret primary documents or materials in relation to their period.

The following topics require, at some point, the task of interpretation:

Analyse in some detail the opening paragraphs of *Bleak House*, concentrating upon the use of language and imagery. (*English*)

Make a critical examination of one article from any issue of the *Edinburgh Review* or the *Quarterly Review* between 1837–1850 which deals with a contemporaneous subject and show what it reveals about early Victorian attitudes. (*history*)

Assess the contemporary significance of Radcliffe-Brown's 1925 paper on the Mother's Brother in South Africa. (*anthropology*)

Planning

It is useful to distinguish between 'planning' (a process) and 'plan' (an outline). 'Planning' takes place from the very beginning as you make choices among topics, as you read and select your material. A 'plan', on the other hand, is an outline of the way you propose to structure your ideas and information.

Plans can be drawn up at various stages of thinking about and writing your essay; planning is a continuous process. You will find that a tentative form of planning begins when you first analyse the topic. Even the way in which you ask yourself questions about the essay establishes some sort of order for collecting and recording information. As you read and take notes you become clearer about what parts the topic naturally falls into, or can reasonably be divided into. You will find yourself beginning to think about the way in which some of these parts relate to one another. Similarly, as you write you will be constantly shifting ideas and information about in your head, and on paper, to see where they fit best: deleting, expanding, writing, planning, rewriting.

Planning is in fact a creative process. It is the process by which you transform:

the demands of the topic,
the ideas of other writers, and
your own thoughts

into your own original argument.

No one way . . .

There are as many styles of planning as there are students writing essays. Here are three students describing the ways in which they work best:

David:
First I begin to read through my notes to get the ideas clear in my head. But this doesn't last long. I get bored going over the same old ground. So, even though I haven't sorted out my ideas, I start writing anyway. It's

only after I've written a few paragraphs that I know clearly what I want to write. Sometimes it's more than that. Longer. It can take hours. But gradually the argument becomes clear as I write. When I've got it straight, I go back . . . Well, it depends. Sometimes I start again with it all clear, and sometimes I continue on to the end. Anyway I find I'm revising as I go because I know what I want to say.

Anna:

I write on coffee. I read over all my notes and then have a cup of coffee or take the dog for a walk. This lets the ideas bubble away at the back of my mind. Then I try and block out on a piece of paper the main points I want to make. I also put down the quotes and references I know for sure I want to use. I mean I put the ideas in the order I think I'll write them in. This is my outline I write from, you know, developing the ideas as I go but still coming back to the outline to check where I'm heading. Between coffee. I stop at each of the main sections and think again about where I'm going next.

Ben:

Well, I'm not so keen on working it out as you go along. I spend a lot of time thinking out the argument before I write a word. I make an outline. No, I make a series of outlines, building up the detail each time. And making the structure clearer. Then when I write, I try and get the first paragraph just right before I go on. Sometimes I work away at it for hours. Not just the same paragraph, but three or four different tries at it, till I think I've got it perfect. Or as good as I can. I do the same with each paragraph. I don't like thinking that when I get to the end I'll have to do the whole thing again. So I revise as I go. That's not always true, though. Sometimes I have to go back to the first paragraph because the argument changed a bit along the way. Mostly try to keep the argument in line on the way through.

In fact all three strategies can be successful, but for different individuals. And it is misleading to suggest that one method is necessarily better than another. The one process that is necessary, and is achieved at different stages in all these approaches, is the *conscious ordering* of the material.

You will notice also that in all three accounts the connection between planning and writing is extremely fluid; that even Ben, who has the most rigidly structured approach, is reshaping his material in the light of what emerges in his writing. In this sense planning and writing are truly interactive, and creative, processes.

General planning strategies

Despite the wide variety of individual styles of planning, there are some strategies which seem generally useful. You may find the following system of working helpful. You can always adapt it as you go.

1 Analyse the essay topic. Check again how you are being directed to handle your material.

2 Read through all your notes. Do this both to remind yourself of material you may have read many weeks before and partially forgotten, and also to get an overview of the material which is now available for your use.

3 Begin to identify key points. There are various things you may wish to do at this stage. You may find it helpful to use the margins of your notes to make cross-references. You may want to underline or highlight points which you now see are important to your argument. Maybe you will write out the key points and quotations on a separate sheet of paper, or cut them out of your pages of notes—and maybe even dump them into separate files on your computer. You could sort your notes into categories depending either on their common content or according to some gradually emerging order. If you are keeping your notes in computer files, you will need at some point to print them out as hard copy so that you can see them 'all at once' and look for connections and relationships between them.

4 Think about a potential order for your material. Give yourself time to think about the significance of the materials you have collected. Think about the various ways in which they could be combined and ordered in relation to the topic. Think about the ways in which these materials seem 'naturally' to fall into a pattern. Think about the central aim of your argument and how your materials could be used to support and develop it.

5 Draw up a tentative plan. Block out on paper at least the main stages of your essay and a tentative conclusion. You may find it useful to include key names or points under each general stage. You may even want to pick out a particular quotation for your starting point. (But remember that this 'plan' is not a rigid guideline. It can be changed once you start writing.)

If you want to see a variety of plans for a common essay topic, then turn to Appendix 5.

Finally, you may be disappointed to discover that there is no single foolproof method of planning your essay. Don't be. It means that you can forget the nagging worry that there is some 'skill' in this whole business of thinking and writing which, if only you can obtain it, will set you up for academic life. In fact, most essay topics do have an inherent structure which emerges, almost spontaneously, as you work through the materials. Each time you write an essay you are faced with the same difficulty of discerning this structure and shaping it to your purposes.

Summary

In this chapter we have looked at the related stages of analysing your essay topic in order to identify what you are directed to do with your material, and of working towards a tentative plan for your essay. We have stressed that planning is a process which takes place continuously throughout the preparation for and drafting of an essay. And that there is no one style of developing a plan which is 'the best'.

The important points to remember are:

1 You need to analyse your topic carefully.
2 Most essays involve both description and analysis.
3 Other common tasks in essays are evaluation of controversy, definition and clarification, and interpretation.
4 Planning is a process by which your ideas, your materials and the demands of the set topic are transformed into an original piece of writing.
5 At some stage in the production of your essay you must develop a conscious plan, but how and when you do this depends on your individual style of working.
6 There are some steps which are useful in developing an essay plan, including close reference to the topic, reading over all your notes, and developing a tentative sequence of content.

Chapter **7**

Drafting and redrafting

All writing involves hard labour: what T.S. Eliot calls the 'intolerable wrestle with words and meanings'.

By the end of secondary school you had probably developed a good system for working on essays. But university essay writing imposes new demands. As we have seen, the topics are more complex, and you are required to do a lot of independent reading and research. In addition, the essays are usually much longer than those you wrote at school, which raises new problems of structuring your material. And there are conventions of style and scholarship (use of bibliographies, references, etc.) which may be unfamiliar. You will need to adjust your system of writing to meet these demands.

For a start, you can no longer get by with only one writing (draft) of an essay. You'll need to write at least two drafts because the first and second drafts are written for different purposes. In the first draft you are writing primarily for *yourself*: writing through the material in order to impose an order on it and to see, at the end of it all, exactly what you think. In the second, and possibly subsequent drafts, you are much more aware of your *reader* —your tutor or lecturer. At this stage you are constantly adjusting the style, tone, presentation and other features of the essay to meet his or her expectations.

Characteristics of academic essay writing

All writing involves a writer, a content and a reader. What distinguishes one type of writing from another is the context in which it takes place. The special characteristics of essay writing in an academic context are shown in the following diagram.

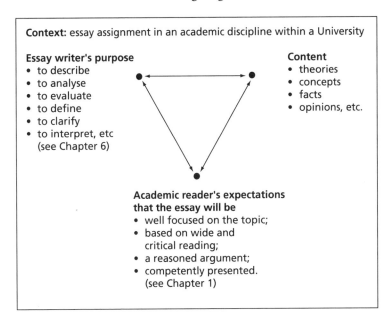

Context: essay assignment in an academic discipline within a University

Essay writer's purpose
- to describe
- to analyse
- to evaluate
- to define
- to clarify
- to interpret, etc
  (see Chapter 6)

Content
- theories
- concepts
- facts
- opinions, etc.

**Academic reader's expectations
that the essay will be**
- well focused on the topic;
- based on wide and
  critical reading;
- a reasoned argument;
- competently presented.
  (see Chapter 1)

Context: You are now writing in a discipline within a university. Therefore you are immediately constrained in terms of your purpose, the content you may use, your voice, style and language. For example, the voice you adopt to present your argument must be a combination of your own personal voice and the specialist voice of the discipline—the voice of the sociologist, the philosopher or the literary critic.

Writer's purpose: As a university student your primary purpose in writing is to present a reasoned argument based on evidence. You might also have a more specific purpose in mind, such as justifying your view that one of Donne's poems is better than another, or that one pricing scheme for medical services is better than others. Also you'll be aiming to get a high mark. But your overriding purpose— presenting a reasoned argument—is governed by the context in which you are writing and your reader's expectations.

Reader's expectations: These have been set out in detail in Chapter 1. There is necessarily a tension between your purposes as a writer and your reader's expectations. You are trying to draw your reader in the direction of your conclusion. The reader, though open to conviction, will be constantly checking the track of your argument for such features as consistency, logic, use of evidence and clarity.

Content: Just as your purpose and your reader's expectations are shaped by context, so too is your content. This content is not the fruit of your naked wit or imagination but the material you have already collected in your reading. Now you must manipulate it and present it in a way that will achieve your purpose.

It is the way in which you shape this material to support your own argument that gives your essay its stamp of 'originality'. You are not expected to discover original material in your reading and research. But you are expected to construct your argument out of the material you do find. In so far as it is your own argument, it is original.

So the quality of your essay will be judged by the extent to which you have satisfactorily balanced these four factors:

- the **context** in which you are writing;
- your **purpose** in writing;
- your **reader's expectations**; and
- your selection, arrangement and presentation of **content**.

The first draft

The first draft involves writing to understand what you think. It is written largely for yourself. This does not mean that you may totally ignore your reader. Rather it means that your primary focus is *inwards* at this stage. You are conscious, above all, of a voice in your own head which is 'thinking aloud': sorting through the material, selecting and rejecting, planning, ordering and rearranging; trying out alternatives for the next words; looking backwards and forwards over the sentence you are presently constructing, seeing if it sounds right, if it says what you are trying to say; wondering how you'll get from the idea you're writing now to the next idea you vaguely know is looming up.

Because you are focused inwards in your first draft, attending to this internal voice which is making sense of your material and fashioning it into an argument, you cannot attend at the same time to the demands of your reader. At this stage you are still sorting out your own ideas. You are not yet ready for anyone else's criticism. In redrafting, you will need to give attention to the most appropriate ways of presenting your argument to your reader. But for the moment concentrate on 'talking' your way, however tentatively, through the whole argument.

In summary, therefore, it is a useful strategy to regard the first draft of your essay as a private matter. This draft is not your last word on the subject. It is not even written for criticism by anyone but yourself. It represents one stage in the development of your ideas. It can, and certainly will, be changed, rearranged and improved. But it is a start.

Stumbling blocks

1 Inability to get started. You'll probably hear your friends complain, 'Starting is the hardest part. If only I can get that right, I can go on.' Some writers scratch away at the first paragraph for hours, searching for the perfect opening. But you shouldn't be aiming at perfection in your first draft of an essay.

Why not try writing the introductory paragraph very quickly, so that you can get on to the real content of your essay before you give up in frustration? At this stage it is important to get your ideas and words flowing. Later you will have to come back and rewrite your introduction anyway, in the light of your conclusion. That will be the time to polish it to your heart's content.

2 Getting stuck part-way through. There will be times when you are stuck, trying to find the right word or a neat way of linking two points. That's inevitable. But there may also be times when you feel totally stuck. You do not know what should come next. This can happen when you have come to the end of one section of your essay and are looking for some way of bridging to the next. Maybe you just need a break. If this doesn't work, try talking the problem over with someone—perhaps a tutor or fellow student. It does not really matter whether the listener is familiar with the subject matter of your essay so long as he or she can ask intelligent questions. Often in the very act of discussing the problem, the solution occurs to you.

If none of this works, go and see your lecturer. He or she may be able to point to some important concept which you have missed altogether or partially misunderstood. Most academics are ready to help if they can see you have really tried to solve the problem for yourself.

3 Finding part-way through that your reading and note-taking have been inadequate. There may be two aspects to this problem: the first resulting from a fundamental gap in your reading; the second from poor planning.

If you become aware that there is a genuine gap in your reading, then you're stuck. You have no real alternative but to go back and do the reading. If, however, the missing material is not essential at this stage (for example, a quotation which you can only vaguely remember but which you know supports your point), then it is safe to continue with your writing and merely note in the margin that something must be looked up and inserted later.

If you find that you are constantly referring back to your notes as you write and—more than that—that you are constantly shuffling through pieces of paper looking for ideas or quotes you half-remember, bits of information you 'know you have somewhere', then your planning has let you down. You'll probably have to take time off and organise your notes and materials more effectively.

4 Your initial argument goes sour or you lose the track. These are two different but related problems. If you suddenly realise that your argument is drying up or that it is going in the wrong direction and your evidence no longer supports it, what can you do? You can just struggle on, hoping your reader will not notice the weakness. Or resign yourself to doing more work. This does not mean that your work so far has been totally wasted. What you have to do is rethink your argument on the basis of these same materials and then replan and rewrite in line with your improved understanding.

The second problem—losing the track of argument—is easier to solve. You must go back to a point in the essay where you are confident about your argument. Then ask yourself 'What should come next?' You can usually pick up quite quickly the point at which you wandered into the side-track. You may, in the course of writing, have been diverted by an idea which is only on the fringe of your essay topic. Or you may have used a relevant example but then chosen an irrelevant point from it to develop as your next step. Whatever the cause of the problem, you must go back until you are on course again.

If none of these strategies works, then again you are in need of outside help.

5 Running out of stamina. Thinking and writing are exhausting. The strategy of taking frequent breaks seems sensible and tempting. On the other hand, you often need to push on and on, uninterrupted, in order to keep up the momentum of your argument. Too many short breaks, or even one long break in the course of the first writing, may disrupt your thinking.

There seems no easy answer to this problem. Writers develop all sorts of individual strategies for coping with it. Some allow themselves frequent breaks but only after they've sketched out the beginning of the next section. Others simply struggle on to the point of exhaustion. Others depend heavily on cigarettes, coffee or chocolate. Others promise themselves rewards once they have finished. You'll have to devise your own strategy for keeping going. Continuity is important in the first writing.

Redrafting

The first draft is complete. You are probably not very happy with it, but it is a relief to have something down on paper. At this stage you need, above all, to distance yourself from your writing. If you can, put the essay away for one or two days. Your mind will continue to turn the ideas over, but more coolly. When you do come back to the essay, you will find it easier to look at it critically.

There is a sound reason for this need to become detached from your argument and material. Until now you have been writing for *yourself*, satisfying yourself about what you think. Now you must shift your focus and begin to consider how to satisfy someone else, the *external* reader and critic. Will my argument satisfy the reader? Is it relevant? Is it logical? Is it clear? Does it flow? Is it well expressed? Does it meet the 'lecturers' expectations' set out in Chapter 1? At this stage you should still only be concerned with questions related to the quality of your thinking and style. The final details of presentation should be left to the later stage of editing (see Chapter 8).

So how can you set about revising your first draft effectively? You could start by asking yourself these two questions about what you've written:

1 Is it *intellectually* convincing?
2 Does it *sound* convincing?

The following checklist should help you to identify those parts of your draft which need redrafting. The lefthand column sets out the questions you need to ask about your argument and style, and the righthand column suggests some practical strategies for finding solutions to these questions. In some cases the strategies are self-explanatory. In others a more detailed explanation is given in the pages which follow the checklist.

Checklist for redrafting

Question 1 Is it intellectually convincing?	Practical strategies for finding solutions
Scope and focus:	
a Is your draft too short or too long?	Expand or prune (see p. 67)
b Have you answered the question?	Skim quickly through your notes.
i Have you answered the whole question?	Read through any outline you have made.
ii Have you answered questions other than the one asked?	Read the draft again, making notes in the margin where changes seem
c Have you covered all of the important areas noted in your reading?	necessary. (You will need to take all of these steps to answer questions b and c satisfactorily.)
Logic and structure:	
d Is there a clear thread of argument running through your essay?	Construct a summary of your argument based on the paragraphs
i Do the separate parts relate logically one to another?	(see p. 67–8).
ii Is there a satisfactory balance in the development of your argument?	Ask another reader for a second opinion.
e Does your essay have an effective introduction and conclusion?	Read the first and last paragraphs and check that they reflect the key concerns of the topic (see pp. 68–74).

Question 2 Does it sound convincing?	Practical strategies for finding solutions
a Is your phrasing precise and accurate?	After your second draft read quickly
b Are the voice and style you adopt:	back over one or two pages from your sources (to reacquaint yourself
i appropriate?	with the voice of the disciplinary
ii consistent?	specialist). Then read your own essay aloud. Ask another reader for a second opinion.

Practical strategies

Question 1 Is it *intellectually* convincing?

1a Is your draft too short or too long?

Variations of approximately 10 per cent above and below the prescribed number of words are generally acceptable. In setting the word limit on an essay, the lecturer is giving an indication of the extent of detail required. If, therefore, you are well over the number of words set, this may be a warning that irrelevant material has crept into your essay or that your style is verbose. (Not always, of course; maybe you have done a great deal more reading than the lecturer expects of average students.) If you are well below the number of words, this may be a signal that you have left out part of the question or an important area of material, or that your style is too clipped.

So, if you find you need to *expand* the number of words:

- See if there is an area of content which you have left out or one which can be expanded.
- See if the general points you are arguing need further evidence or more detailed examples.
- See if your essay needs more detailed background information on which to base your analysis. You may be assuming that your reader's knowledge of your material is greater than in fact it is.
- See if you need to make your argument clearer for your reader by making the links in your reasoning more explicit.

If you find you need to *reduce* the number of words:

- Look for irrelevancies and repetitions, and prune vigorously.
- Look for lists of evidence and examples which could be covered by a brief generalisation.
- Look for explanation, background and assumptions which may be cut out or covered by a reference.

1d Is there a clear thread of argument running through your essay?

i Do the separate parts relate logically one to another?
ii Is there a satisfactory balance in the development of your argument?
  Read through your draft, asking yourself at the end of each paragraph: 'What is the main point in this paragraph?' Then write a

one sentence *summary* of each of your paragraphs. This summary is valuable: it tells you what you *have* said, which may be surprisingly different from what you *intended to say*. It will soon show you:

- whether your argument is consistent;
- whether the connection between one point and another is clear;
- whether your ideas are in the right order;
- whether your ideas are organised into paragraph units;
- whether one section is unnecessarily long (maybe the opening section?);
- whether the discussion of theory and concepts is adequately balanced by the use of examples;
- whether one aspect is treated in much greater detail than another (is this justifiable?).

In some of your essays you may gratefully recognise that little renovation is necessary because the essay, as it stands, is reasonably well organised and clear. Other essays may require much greater reorganisation because your thoughts and your material only gradually took shape as you were in the process of writing. Most commonly you will find that some sections of your essay are almost totally acceptable and need only minor revisions, and other sections need much more drastic rewriting.

There may be times when you feel so unsure of your own judgement about the quality of your draft that you want to get a *second opinion*. This is a sensible strategy. Don't be hesitant about using it. Some students feel reluctant to ask other people to read a draft of their essay, maybe because they feel ashamed of it, or don't want to waste other people's time, or feel it is somehow 'cheating'. But you are not asking anyone to write the essay for you. You are merely asking for constructive criticism. You are doing what all academics do with their own writing. It is one of the best ways of testing out and clarifying ideas.

Appendix 6 contains an example of one student's attempts to reorganise a first draft.

1e Does your essay have an effective introduction and conclusion?

Why do essay writers find the first and last paragraphs of an essay so difficult? 'If only I could get my introduction straight, then I could go on.' 'My conclusion just seems to repeat the opening.' 'What are you supposed to do in a conclusion anyway?' 'What do they mean "round off" your essay?' 'How can I be original and dramatic in the opening?'

The introduction and conclusion are key points in your essay; maybe that is why you feel so reluctant about writing them. First and last impressions do matter. So what should these paragraphs include?

Introduction

Let's begin by looking at what some students actually do in writing a first paragraph. Compare these two openings which appear to have the same general purpose; that is, to strike a note of warning about the uncritical use of certain source materials.

Example 1, political science topic:
'Compare and discuss the accounts by Kelly, Oakes, and Reid of the [Australian] Governor-General's dismissal of the Whitlam government on 11 November 1975.'

Opening: Certainly, it would be extremely difficult to consider and discuss three accounts of the one event without giving something of a book review, without repeating what must have been said by many others and remaining impartial towards those accounts. Logically, there must be the same difficulties involved when the authors go to present the facts in the first place. It is a human attribute that could not be expected to be suppressed.

Example 2, prehistory topic:
'Discuss the ways in which studies of a contemporary hunter-gatherer group may help us to understand the archaeological record. Apply to a contemporary hunter-gatherer group.'

Opening: If observations of living groups are to be of use in helping us to reconstruct prehistoric life-ways, great care must be taken when interpreting the ethnographic evidence. It is a risky business to assume that because certain socio-cultural patterns are apparent in modern groups, that these must have parallels in their prehistoric equivalents.

The differences are striking. Example 2 is a clear, though carefully qualified, statement that there are 'risks' in drawing inferences about prehistory from contemporary human societies. It seems that the writer intends to look especially at 'socio-cultural patterns', and you would be justified in expecting her to make explicit, with examples, just what those risks are. In other words, you have been given some understanding of the writer's point of view and you have some indication of the area in which she intends to apply it. Example 1, by contrast, fails to make a clear and comprehensive statement about the topic. The long first sentence is about the writer himself and his difficulties in coming to terms with the task, rather than an explicit statement about the task itself. The one substantial point suggested at the end of the paragraph is that facts are always presented within an interpretative framework. This is an important point, but it is only implicit and not clearly directed to the topic. At the end of the paragraph we are still unsure of what the writer is going to argue in his essay.

Two more examples of introductions, this time both for the same topic, are discussed in Appendix 7.

Look now at an opening paragraph from an essay in a Greek civilisation course. The lecturer's comment on this was: 'A superb introduction: clear, intelligent, and perceptive'.

Example 3, Greek history topic:
Fifth century Athens is usually considered to have been the birthplace of 'democracy', but the term 'democracy' has come to have a variety of connotations. Discuss the nature of Athenian democracy of the 5th century B.C.: its ideals and its actual workings. (Useful comparisons or contrasts with modern democracy will be welcomed but are not obligatory. Beware of unsupported generalisations.)

Opening: The Athenian constitution of the fifth century was remarkable for the democratic principles it embodied—hitherto unheard of. The ideals of any society are difficult to evaluate without over-simplification; however, four main principles can be discerned in fifth century Athens: sovereignty of the citizens, equality, liberty, and justice for the citizens. A greater insight into the nature of the democracy can be achieved by examination of its more important institutions: the Assembly, electoral eligibility, electoral method, duration of office, ostracism and the liturgies. This century some have disputed the validity of Athenian democracy, one reason being the exclusion of women, metics, and slaves from participating in government. However, the difference between fifth century Athenian government and a Western twentieth century democracy lies not essentially in the theory behind the constitution but in the definition of a citizen.

Here you have been given an impression of the probable development of the whole essay: a discussion of the nature of Athenian democracy, looking at its principles and its major institutions; then an examination of modern criticisms of the political system; and, finally, some comparison between Athenian democracy and modern theories of democracy. Notice also how skilfully the writer has suggested the order in which she will develop her ideas, without explicitly saying 'First', 'Second', 'Third', 'Next', 'Finally', etc.

Your reaction to the Athenian democracy essay may have been: 'I wonder if I could write an opening as clear as that'. In fact you could—but only with practice, and only if you understand what the special tasks of the introductory paragraph are. From the discussion of actual examples here and in Appendix 7, you can recognise two of these tasks:

1 Your first paragraph should focus your reader's attention on the central themes of your essay and express a clear point of view.
2 It should give the reader some understanding of the order in which you are going to develop your ideas.

These are essential tasks. You may sometimes also want to do other things, such as define a central term or concept, or use a key quotation as a starting point. It is usually only when you have completed your first draft that you can see clearly what needs to go into your first paragraph. Even then, it may take you two or three revisions to create an opening that really satisfies you.

For an example of the stages of redrafting one student went through in writing her introductory paragraph, see Appendix 8.

Conclusion

Your essay cannot merely come to a stop. You must draw it to a conclusion. In the body of the essay you have been developing your argument in detail. The concluding paragraph must pull together all of those details into a general statement which sums up your argument. It should refer your reader back to the topic. This gives your essay a sense of unity.

Note that 'summing up your argument' implies more than simply summarising or repeating your point of view. A conclusion needs to answer the question 'So what?'—so what does all this analysis and evidence add up to? So how are we to evaluate the controversy your essay has dealt with? So what do you want to persuade your reader to think about the issues discussed?

Because it is your final word on the topic, the last paragraph can make a great impact on the reader. This potential impact will probably be lost if:

1 The final paragraph merely presents the development of a minor point in your argument—for example, this conclusion to a sociology essay comparing the structures of group and sub-group norms:

Example 4
Having shown the importance of the external system and interaction upon sub-group development, I now finish with another allusion to the negative

effect of an absence of interaction. The researchers were able to perceive that the group studied, the isolated group, were being treated with increasing antagonism by the rest of the department and, true to form, they perceived themselves as an isolated unit within which they must seek identification.

2 The paragraph ends with a lengthy quotation, which may mean that you have been working towards someone else's conclusion—for example, this conclusion to an anthropology essay on distinctions between tribal, peasant and modern societies:

Example 5
Other traditional structures persist, as noted by C. Nakani (1967, p. 172):

> 'Many particular aspects ... disappearing from rural life today, owing to expansion of industrialisation. However, the distinctive characteristics of Japanese social structure . . . in their rural milieu are, in my view, persisting in various modern communities such as factories, business firms, schools, intellectual groups, political parties, etc . . .'

3 The paragraph is so cryptic as to be 'clever' without depth—for example, this concluding two sentence paragraph of an anthropology essay on the nature of 'exchange' in Aboriginal society:

Example 6
The basis of exchange is many things and no single thing. The best we can say is that the basis of exchange is a dialogue acted on a cultural stage.

While your conclusion is shaped by the need to reacquaint your reader with the major themes of the essay and your overall point of view, the actual strategies for concluding may be as varied as those introductory strategies we examined earlier. Here, for example, is a conclusion which seems to work well. The writer not only takes us back to the central terms of the topic but also makes clear that his exploration of the topic has led him to a re-definition of it. The central question of slavery, he suggests, is never one of relative degrees of humanity but of relative degrees of economic advantage to the slavers.

Example 7
Topic: What were the unique features of slavery in the British North American colonies, as contrasted with slavery in the French, Spanish, and Portuguese colonies? Under which colonial slave system would it have been preferable to be a slave?

Conclusion: So the question of which was the preferable slave system is really unanswerable. It would depend on what was of prime importance to the individual, the greater chance of legally acquiring his freedom or the stronger possibility of survival. In practical terms the overall deciding factor in the actual treatment of slaves was the economic one. In French, Spanish and Portuguese colonies it was cheaper to replenish stocks of slaves by purchasing rather than breeding them. In North America it was generally found a better policy to look after the slaves one had and to foster their breeding. In the long term 'humane' slave codes provide protection against the greed of the master.

Another strategy is simply to refer to a key word or phrase in your introduction. Or you can relate the structure of your conclusion to the structure of your opening. Here is an example of this technique from a student's history essay:

Example 8
Topic: What did the work of Caroline Chisholm do for the position of women in Colonial Society?

Opening: The philanthropic works of Caroline Chisholm in the 19th century were held in high esteem by her contemporaries. She was known as the messenger of mercy, a benefactress, and as a redresser of female wrongs. Mrs Chisholm was no radical and undertook this work purely on humanitarian grounds. Her dearest wish, after helping immigrant young women on arrival in the colony of New South Wales, was that they should marry and procreate, thus establishing the family as a stabilising influence in that untamed land. She firmly believed that wives and children—God's police—would bring about a new society. There is no doubt that Mrs Chisholm elevated the position of women by her deeds. By sheltering these young women on arrival at Sydney and finding them employment she no doubt saved many from a questionable fate. Her presence at the wharves and the realisation that someone cared about their welfare must surely have given hope to many a destitute girl. Yet, as good as her intentions were, was not Mrs Chisholm merely moving these women from one role and placing them in another? Were they not by becoming wives and mothers still chattels without any identity or independence—merely an object for a husband's whims? One stereotype replacing another?

Conclusion: The answer to the question: 'What did Caroline Chisholm's work do for the position of colonial woman?' is twofold. Through her love of mankind she endeavoured to make life better for women in the way she and her generation understood. Her unceasing efforts to help young immigrant women who were abandoned in Sydney by providing them with love, food, shelter and employment was the first step. Her perseverance with government officials to gain help and point out injustices must have helped the women's plight. By her faith and determination—which she believed was derived from divine inspiration—by her understanding of the needs of the women in the colony, and by great personal sacrifice, Caroline Chisholm did much to raise the accepted standard of women in colonial society. By preventing exploitation of the immigrant women on arrival at Sydney, she offered these young women an independence that was needed to lift their class. Unfortunately she only anticipated this independence as transitional to the ultimate goal of marriage. Marriage, like whoredom, can also be experienced as a yoke around the neck. Women were placed in this new role under men's terms. They were to be at the beck and call of their husbands and children with all independence, identity and originality stripped from them. It is ironic that in the process of shaking off one stigma they had taken on another. Perhaps the price to pay was too great?

The opening paragraph begins, appropriately, with the writer placing her subject in an historical context. She then sketches the basis for contemporary views of Caroline Chisholm's work. Finally, (the conjunction 'yet' signals a change in direction) the writer raises a number of questions, suggesting the need for a reassessment of Caroline Chisholm's work.

The concluding paragraph closely reflects the structure of the introduction, though there are subtle differences in the strength of the views advanced in each. The first half of the paragraph affirms contemporary views of Caroline Chisholm. That part of the case, at least, has been established. The second half of the paragraph firmly answers the questions raised in the second half of the introduction. The writer concludes that Caroline Chisholm was an agent of another, more subtle, exploitation than the one she attacked. By creating a conclusion which reflects so closely the structure and central themes of her introduction, this writer has given the whole essay a sense of unity and completeness.

Question 2 Does it *sound* convincing?

2b Are the voice and style you adopt:
    i   appropriate, and
    ii consistent?

'Style' may be used to describe a particular type of writing distinguished by its function or context (legal style), or to refer to some general features of writing (clarity is 'good style').

When you get an essay back covered with such comments as 'Poor expression', 'Awful!', 'Cliche', 'Jargon', 'A bit pompous?', your lecturer has been irritated by your style. How can you improve it? What is 'academic style' anyway?

At the beginning of this chapter there was a diagram showing the relationship between writer's purpose, reader's expectations, content, and the context of writing. The distinctive features of academic style are closely related to these four factors. For example, in an academic context language is used to express analytical and abstract thinking. For this reason you will find lengthier and more complex paragraphs and sentences in an academic paper than in, say, an army instruction manual. The purpose of the manual is to issue instructions; lengthy complex sentences are not the best means of doing this.

Let us tackle this matter of distinctive styles in a more practical way. Read this paragraph from an academic journal:

Extract 1
What are the anatomical bases for the human communication system? Asymmetry of the brain has been linked with language and speech and was once considered a distinguishing feature of the human neocortex. But recent research shows that there is possible asymmetry in the cortex of great apes (orangutan and chimpanzees).[1] Hemispheric asymmetry implies specialisation of function; coordination and integration therefore become critical. The size of the corpus callosum, a bundle of nerve-fibers connecting the right and left hemispheres, is consistent with the possibility of some hemispheric asymmetry for the great apes. This structure is relatively (and absolutely) large in humans; next in apes, then in monkeys, its volume (compared to the medulla) is 1.2 to 1 for monkeys, 1.8 to 1 for chimpanzees and 3 to 1 for humans.[2] In addition to investigating the anatomical bases, viewing communication in a social context with brain-behaviour interrelationships is an approach that will assist in integrating many types of data.

What is it about this paragraph that is distinctively academic in style? Certainly the content. And, linked with content, the use of specialist terms; for example, neocortex, corpus callosum. What else? Perhaps the cautiousness with which claims are made? 'But recent research shows . . . *possible* asymmetry . . .', 'The size of the corpus callosum . . . is consistent with the *possibility* of . . .' The tone of the passage is very cool and detached. The writer is somewhat distanced from the material he is evaluating. Look too at the writer's concern for providing evidence, both within the text and through references, in support of the points he makes. This concern for evidence and objectivity of tone can lead to some very long and complex structures; look, for example, at the last sentence. Above all, there is a sense of a mind and voice moving steadily through the material: persuasive but distanced.

Consider the contrasting style of this passage in which a well-known Australian novelist gives some advice about drafting to fellow writers:

Extract 2

I've worked this over three times you know, the writer on the phone complains emphatically, as though such a huge effort is totally beyond the call of duty. I try to cheer him up by saying I've been working on my piece for more than a year, that I've had the idea brewing up for more than five, that at the moment, I'm up to draft number fourteen. But he obviously doesn't believe me. How could anyone, these days, possibly do more than three drafts? We've got deadlines as well as mortgages to meet. Any investment of time has to return a profit. Three drafts is his absolute limit. And that is more than he would usually do.

Whatever happened to the draft process? Whatever happened to Joseph Conrad's idea of putting away a manuscript for a year before attempting a revision? Whatever happened to James Joyce's idea that a whole day spent perfecting one sentence was a worthy expenditure of time and effort?

Speed and volume are the virtues of the day. The faster, the bigger, the better. A certain well-known writer prides herself on the fact that she writes a minimum of 1500 words a day, like a ringer boasting about his sheep-shearing tally. Creative writing workshops are held to train people how to write fast, as though writers will some day be entered into the Olympics and their literary abilities measured in nanoseconds.

Yes, yes, I know as well as any freelance writer, that to make a living, you have to write fast. You have to produce. But perhaps there needs to be some distinction between different types of production.

Journalism, by its nature, needs to be written quickly. But novels? Essays? Short stories?

How would you describe the tone of voice here? Is it distant and dispassionate, or familiar and passionate? Objective or intensely involved? Does the writer provide evidence for her viewpoint and assertions? What kinds of evidence (paras 2 and 3)? What kinds of questions does she ask (para 2)? Is the vocabulary 'specialised' in any way? In what context would we normally expect to find paragraphs and sentences of this length? Are there any other ways in which this passage—however well written—is different in style from Extract 1?

From this contrast you can recognise some characteristics of academic style. The academic writer's *approach* to his or her material is:

analytical		impressionistic
objective	*rather than*	subjective
intellectual		emotional
rational		polemical

The academic writer's *tone* is:

serious		conversational
impersonal	*rather than*	personal
formal		colloquial

The academic writer makes frequent use of:

- passive forms of the verb
- impersonal pronouns and phrases
- qualifying words and phrases
- complex sentence structures
- specialised vocabulary

Check if you can identify some of these features of academic style in another passage; see Appendix 9.

In drawing attention to these characteristics of academic style, we are not suggesting that this is necessarily 'good' style. We are not saying, for example, that impersonal and passive forms, e.g. 'It may be inferred that . . .' are more effective than personal and active forms, e.g. 'I infer that . . .' We are saying that the former are standard usage for much academic writing and therefore need to be learned and used when appropriate.

Differences between disciplines

So far we have isolated some of the common characteristics of academic style. You will soon realise, if you are studying in more than one discipline, that there are differences in style between disciplines as well as between academic and other forms of writing. Read the three following paragraphs and see if you can identify the disciplines from which they have been taken:

Extract 3
Exploratory tendencies evident in many animals seem also to reflect a preference for novelty or for increments in stimulation. Animals tend to explore actively any novel environment that permits more exploration over one that permits less. Moreover, animals will learn a response that

is rewarded by the opportunity to explore. Rats choose the arm of a Y-maze that leads to a checkerboard maze over one that leads to a blind alley. Exploratory tendencies appear to be independent of general activity, and their occurrence does not require the accompanying state of deprivation that is characteristic of the regulatory drives such as hunger or thirst.

Extract 4

Our last example concerns the use of pronouns in BEV. Bereiter and Engelmann found that BEV speakers left out relative pronouns ('This here is one family eat nothing') but that they did use pronouns pleonastically ('My sister *she* play piano'). It is a part of their compensatory programme to adapt BEV children to the norms of pronoun use in SE. As Smith (1969) has already shown, however, such a measure would bring the child into verbal conflict. The reason for this is that there is a close correlation between the omission of the relative pronoun in BEV and the pleonastic use of the subject pronoun. In such sentences where the relative pronoun is omitted, the pleonastic pronoun is applied to remove any ambiguities. If, therefore, the programme of Bereiter and Engelmann is supposed to teach the children to omit the pleonastic pronoun, this will cause communicative interference within BEV usage.

Extract 5

But what one makes of the ending of the play depends on what one makes of the Duke; and I am embarrassed about proceeding, since the Duke has been very adequately dealt with by Wilson Knight, whose essay Knights refers to. The Duke, it is important to note, was invented by Shakespeare: In *Promos and Cassandra*, Shakespeare's source, there is no equivalent. He, his delegation of authority and his disguise (themselves familiar romantic conventions) are the means by which Shakespeare transforms a romantic comedy into a completely and profoundly serious 'criticism of life'. The more-than-Prospero of the play, it is the Duke who initiates and controls the experimental demonstration—the controlled experiment—that forms the action.

You may have been able to identify them as coming from the disciplines of psychology, linguistics (more exactly, sociolinguistics) and literary criticism respectively. There are a number of clues you may have used:

1 Content: Running rats through mazes to test behaviour patterns is a standard psychological experiment; the other two extracts are equally unambiguous in their content.

2 Vocabulary: Each discipline has its own technical language or jargon: 'drive', 'response', 'reward', 'stimulation' typically belong to psychological language (though they are also used in different senses, in common speech); 'pleonastic pronouns', 'communicative interference', 'BEV' (Black English Vernacular) are part of the standard jargon of linguistics. Is there any jargon in Extract 5?

3 Special interest: Extract 5 is exploring the value or quality of the writing of Shakespeare and the justice of other writers' judgements upon him. This is the special interest of literary criticism. Extract 4 is not interested in questions of the aesthetic quality of language but in understanding in a scientific sense the way in which different groups in a community learn and use language. This is one of the special interests of sociolinguistics. What special interest is evident in Extract 3?

You might have noticed some other differences. Extract 5, for example, uses a *personal* form ('I am embarrassed . . .') whereas the other extracts do not. This personal usage is permissible in literary criticism in which there is a greater degree of reliance on subjective response as the basis of argument than in other disciplines. This is not to suggest that it is simply a matter of assertion of opinion. You will notice the writer of Extract 5, in the same way as the sociolinguistic extract, is framing his argument in terms of other writers, critics or sources. Thus the writer measures his own response to the play against those of two other literary critics. All become part of the texture of the writer's own argument about the value of Shakespeare's writing. In a similar way, Smith's criticism of Bereiter and Engelmann is part of the sociolinguist's justification for his own argument. The same general academic method is at work in all the passages.

We started the previous section by asking: are the voice and style you adopt (i) appropriate, and (ii) consistent? We have tried to show what is 'appropriate' by sketching some common features of academic style and by pointing to some differences between disciplines. There is no quick or easy way of mastering these characteristics of style. That takes understanding, concentration, and a concern for detail—and it takes time. You will get better at it:

• the more you read in your disciplines;
• the more you listen to lectures and take part in tutorials and seminars;
• the more closely you attend to the criticisms and comments made on your essays and assignments.

Summary

In this chapter we have tried to analyse what is involved in the central intellectual task of drafting and redrafting your essay. We have looked at some of the common problems which essay writers experience and suggested some strategies for overcoming them.

The important points to remember are:

1 You will need to write at least two drafts of each essay.
2 Your first draft is written for yourself, in order to establish exactly what you think; subsequent drafts are written for an external reader, and your material and style need to be tailored accordingly.
3 Your essay is the result of a balance struck between your own purposes in writing, your content, your reader's expectations, and the context in which you are writing.
4 You will need to develop strategies for overcoming those problems you experience in writing a first draft; for example, being unable to get started or losing the track of your argument.
5 Your redrafting should be based on two major questions:
   • Is the essay intellectually convincing?
   • Does it sound convincing?
6 You should apply to your own writing the criteria of logic and coherence at the paragraph level which were explored in the earlier chapter on reading. In particular, you should give attention to the special functions of the introductory and concluding paragraphs.
7 You should be aware of the characteristic features of academic style.
8 You should also be aware that there are differences in style and usage between disciplines.

Chapter 8

Editing

Now you are ready to write out, or wordprocess, the final version of your essay and hand it in. In this final writing you may still be tinkering with a few sentences; trying to improve the flow, emphasise a shift in thought, qualify a generalisation. But in general you will not now be making any substantial changes or extensions to your argument. At this stage of working on your essay a third question becomes important:

Does it *look* convincing?

You are now working over your essay in the role of editor or proofreader, concerned with the surface presentation rather than the content. You may resent the necessity to spend time on superficial details, especially after your much weightier struggles with ideas and language. Yet presentation is an important element in the persuasiveness of your case. If there are signs of inaccuracy and carelessness at the surface level of your essay, these will invite superficial criticisms from your reader—and may well distract him or her from a more serious consideration of the real argument you have struggled to present. This is the one stage in the whole process of essay writing where there is only one way to be 'correct' and where the criteria for 'correctness' are objective and are based on commonly accepted conventions and practices.

In Chapter 7 we used a checklist to identify the main points to be considered in the drafting stages of the essay. The controlling questions in that checklist were:

Is it *intellectually* convincing?

Does it *sound* convincing?

The practical strategies you used there were largely matters of *judgement*. In this final stage of editing, however, the practical strategies involve strict application of rules and conventions. Now look over this checklist for the final editing stage.

Checklist for editing essays

Question: Does it *look* convincing?	Practical strategies for finding solutions
1 Have you observed the official departmental requirements for the *format* of the essay: • what size paper? • do you write on one side only? • what size margins? • if you are typing, should you use double–spacing? • what must be included on the title page? • is an abstract/synopsis/summary required?	Reread the departmental handout on essay presentation and any particular instructions given for this essay.
2 Is your writing *correct* at the surface level of: • spelling? • punctuation? • grammar? Is it legible?	Read the essay carefully one final time, or ask a reliable friend to proofread it for you. Consult a dictionary or a standard reference book. (See Appendix 12 for a list of useful references, and use computer aids for spelling and grammar checks.)
3 Are the *quotations* you have used: • accurate? • acknowledged? • correctly set out? • fully incorporated into the grammar of your own text?	Check any instructions in departmental handouts about the use of quotations. Read aloud the passages in your essay which include direct quotations and listen to see if they fit in smoothly. If you are unsure about how to handle quotations, see Appendix 13.

Question: Does it *look* convincing?	Practical strategies for finding solutions
4 Are your *references* accurate and correctly set out?	Check departmental handouts. See Appendix 14 for some common referencing styles.
5 Is your *bibliography* accurate and correctly set out?	Check departmental handouts. A common model is provided in Appendix 15.
6 If a *synopsis* is required, is it in the correct style?	Reread instructions for essay. The art of constructing a synopsis/abstract/summary is discussed later in this chapter.

Practical strategies

Here are some additional comments on the checklist.

Essay format

1 Margins: It is important to leave margins which give your lecturer sufficient space in which to write comments as he or she reads your essay. If you do not, then you will be irritating your reader and you will not get feedback on the details of your work.

2 Title page: Some lecturers insist on a specific format for the cover or title page for your assignment: for example, it may be mandatory that you put your name on the back of the last page and not on the front page. If there are no instructions, then it is customary to include (in whatever format you find most pleasing):

- the essay title in full in the exact words in which it is set by the lecturer (*not* your version of the topic);
- the name of the lecturer/tutor to whom you are submitting the essay;
- the name of the course;
- your own name, with an address or contact phone number;
- the date on which you are submitting the essay;
- the approximate number of words in the final essay (not including appendices and footnotes).

Correct use of language

1 Spelling: If you know you are a weak speller, try to get a friend to read over your final draft and pencil in corrections. It is not 'cheating' to get editing assistance; just good sense. There may be ways in which you can improve your spelling ability, but you will almost certainly have exhausted these possibilities already in the earlier stages of your schooling. Some students find it useful to make lists of frequently misspelt words and stick them on the wall in front of their desk. Make use of computer aids such as spellchecks, but don't become over-reliant on them. Remember, spellchecks will not be able to tell you whether the word you actually want is 'there' or 'their'.

2 Expression: If your past essays have been criticised for 'awkward expression', it may help to read *aloud* your final draft. Many students find they can hear mistakes which they cannot pick up merely by looking at the written text.

You should also make a habit of consulting standard reference texts for grammar, punctuation and correct usage.

Quotations

1 Format and referencing: Whenever you copy a passage, word for word, from the work of some other writer, you are quoting. Then you must indicate the quotation by (i) using a special format (either inverted commas for a short quotation, or indentation for a quotation longer than three lines), and by (ii) giving an exact page reference to the source from which you have copied the passage (see Appendices 13 and 14). If you do not indicate quoted passages in this way, you may be accused of *plagiarism*—that is, the unattributed use of the words and work of other writers. At all points in your essay your reader should be aware of a distinction between the ideas, arguments and actual words you have taken from sources, and your own commentary on these.

2 Usage: There is no rule for when or how much you should quote. In some disciplines, such as literary criticism, you may need to quote constantly; in others it may be enough to summarise or make reference to a source. In general, check that your quotations are:

• used sparingly;
• focused precisely on the point you are making;

- brief and telling;
- properly integrated into the flow of your argument and the grammar of your own sentences.

Once you have used a quotation, avoid restating it in your own words. The quotation must play its own part in advancing your argument.

References

In an essay whenever you are:

- quoting the exact words of another writer;
- closely summarising a passage from another writer;
- using an idea or material which is directly based on the work of another writer;

then you must acknowledge your source.

The three most common referencing styles for printed materials are:

1 Footnotes: numbers in the body of the text, following each reference, and numbered acknowledgments of the sources at the bottom of each page. This has the advantage of making it easy for the reader to identify a source at a glance. (For more detail, see Appendix 14.)

2 Endnotes: numbers in the text, but running consecutively through-out the whole essay, and the numbered acknowledgements given in a list at the end of the essay. This permits you to give extended commentaries and additional information about points in your essay.

3 Included references: The minimum information necessary to identify the source is given in brackets in the body of the essay: usually the author's name, date of publication and page number(s). Full details of the printed source are obtained through reference to the Bibliography. This format is common in science and the social sciences.

Bibliography

This is a list of all the sources (printed and electronic) you have found useful during your preparation for the essay—not merely a list of the sources you have actually referred to in the final essay. It is arranged alphabetically, by surname of author, and must have a consistent format. (See Appendix 15.)

In science essays it is usual to give a list of **References** which contains only the sources you have actually cited in the body of your essay.

Synopsis

In some courses, especially in science and the social sciences, you may be required to provide a synopsis (or abstract or summary). This should cover only the outline of your argument (not the details) and the general conclusions you have reached. If the length of the synopsis is not specified, it is usual to aim at a word total of approximately 5–10 per cent of the length of the essay itself.

The synopsis is placed following the title page and in front of the actual essay, so that your reader can see in advance the whole sweep of your argument and the conclusions which you are going to present.

In fact you will write your synopsis *after* you have completed your essay. It is a summary of what you have written, not a blueprint of what you intend to write. For this reason it is customary to write the summary in the present, not the future, tense.

Many academic journals require writers to provide a synopsis or abstract at the head of their article and you can find plenty of examples merely by leafing through journals in your discipline. Here is an example taken from the *British Journal of Psychology* ([1966] 57, 3 and 4, p. 361):

Transfer in Category Learning of Young Children: Its Relation to Task Complexity and Overlearning

By Ann M. Clarke and G.M. Cooper
Department of Psychology, The University of Hull

An investigation with normal pre-school children is reported which confirms and extends earlier findings on subnormal subjects. That transfer is related to the complexity of intervening training is again demonstrated across widely different tasks. In addition, evidence is offered for the interaction of overlearning with complexity, and the possible relevance of transfer in cognitive development is briefly discussed.

And here is an example of a synopsis by a student in a history course:

In this essay the small volume entitled *Sidelights on Two Referendums, 1916–1917* is evaluated as a potential source for an Australian historian. Two of the recurrent themes in the book—humanist antiwar philosophies and the Censorship—are taken as test pieces and, by comparison with parallel sources, an estimate of the author's reliability is gauged.

The conclusion reached is that while the author appears to be a reliable reporter of events, she declines to comment at all on some of the momentous events of the period and therefore this little work is not a very useful source for the historian. However we are given some valuable insights into the personality and philosophy of H.E. Boote, editor of the *Australian Worker* during the conscription referendums.

Wordprocessing

Many students are now writing their essays and reports on computers. The advantages of wordprocessing are obvious: you can rewrite parts of your essay that you are unhappy with easily and quickly; you can shift whole blocks of material around if you don't like the initial organisation of your ideas; you can apply a range of programmed aids and checks (such as spellcheck, grammar check, word count) to what you have written; and you can edit and polish your language to your heart's content—without the bother of having to retype whole pages for perfect presentation.

But all new technologies bring problems as well as benefits. There are three very common pitfalls with wordprocessing. First, some writers have a tendency to become mesmerised by their screens. Thus they produce essays with paragraphs all of the same size, not because their argument or material requires such conformity but because their paragraphs have been shaped to correspond exactly with the size of the screen.

Second, and relatedly, some writers are tempted to polish and perfect single paragraphs (often the opening ones) rather than getting on with the job of developing the whole essay. Having polished and perfected these single paragraphs, they are then reluctant to make the changes that are needed once the draft is complete.

Third, because it is so easy to move sentences and paragraphs (cut and paste), some writers lose track of their argument and sometimes even repeat passages. It is also easy in this cutting and pasting for references to sources to 'drop out'. You can then lay yourself open to charges of plagiarism, and the excuse 'But my machine did it!' is rarely accepted.

Our advice is that it is usually better to push on and complete the draft, then **print out** and do your editing on the hard copy before you enter the changes into the computer. It is vitally important for the structure and coherence of your essay that you see the whole essay as one piece and not just as it rolls past your eye or in separate screenfuls of print.

Summary

In this chapter we have provided a practical checklist to cover those aspects of your final draft which need special attention in editing.

The main points to remember are:

1 Your final essay must be as accurate as possible in details of presentation.
2 You should always check the specific requirements of the department about essay presentation.
3 You should know how to handle quotations, referencing of sources, format for bibliographies, and other requirements of presentation.
4 You may find it useful to ask a friend to read over the final version of your essay in order to pick up errors.
5 If you are writing on a computer, write a complete draft before polishing, and print out the essay so that you can analyse its structure and coherence as a whole.

Chapter 9

Assessment and follow-up

At last it's finished. Your essay has been handed in, and there is nothing more you can do about it. You may simply feel relieved—'I just couldn't do any more with it.' 'I was sick to death of it.' 'I just wanted to get rid of it.' 'Once I'd submitted it, I felt as if a great weight had been lifted off my back.' Or your relief may be tinged with anxiety—'I know it's not perfect, but I think it's more or less all right.' 'What mark will I get?' 'It's only when I get it back that I'll know how good it was, how good the lecturer thought it was.' Yet is this the end of the whole process? What more can you learn from what you have done? There is more to assessment than the final grade.

There are three points at which you can start analysing how effectively you handled the process of writing in that essay:

- the formal assessment by your lecturer;
- your self-assessment;
- discussion with other students.

Feedback from lecturers

The formal assessment of your work may be of three kinds: letter grade or numerical mark; written comments; and direct discussion.

1 Grade or mark: Your immediate reaction, on getting back your essay, is probably to look first for the grade it was given. This represents the 'official' judgement on your performance and is an evaluation both of the quality of your work and the way in which it compares with the work of other students. Of course, this grade is not the final judgement on your intellectual capacities; but it is some indication of your current performance.

Macbeth, when he learns that Fleance 'is scaped' (line 18) and hence that he has not forestalled the witches' second prophesy, is '..' cabined, cribbed, confinded, bound in/To saucy doubts and fears.' (lines 23–24), the <u>tone</u>, <u>rhythym</u> and <u>imagery</u> which the words create <u>show clearly</u>. what he is thinking, and they also tell *of* his character and how he can be trapped by his own thoughts. There is also, in this scene a contrast between Macbeth's apparently orderly front when he is trying to make his Lords feel all is well and the *u* turmoil his mind is in when the ghost appears. This seems to make one feel that Macbeth is really in the grip of something he cannot control. And so perhaps the ghost, although it may be real, is made more real, a horribly powerful and disorderly force, by Macbeth's own fretted mind. It is this aspect of his character which seems to be his downfall, his mind is a prey to his imagination. With 'Which of you has done this' *(line 47)* when he sees the ghost for the first time he becomes divorced from the present, perhaps from reality, and totally absorbed in the horror, of his deeds and the supernatural which has such a destructive force on him. *effect?* As the ghost itself exits and enters, dramatic effectiveness is built up not only on stage but also in the audience, *and?* one feels pulled in to the action.

You must be more specific.

which is?

In combination with his ambition, his vulnerability to the supernatural and his wife's initial manipulations.

I don't see the connection between your quotation and your assertion

You should organise material more effectively. Instead of commenting on dramatic effectiveness at this point, you ought to conitnue discussing Macbeth's state of mind.

2 Written comments: Most commonly your lecturer will write comments on your essay, as well as giving you a final grade. There will be comments in the margin, mainly concerned with details at the sentence level, and a more extended end comment focusing on the whole essay and possibly suggesting strategies for improvement in the next essay.

Let us look at an example of each type of comment. First, here is a paragraph from an English essay on a scene from *Macbeth*. The essay was written by a first-year student and commented on in detail by the marker:

And here is an example of a detailed end comment on a first-year essay in European Literature and Society (1789–1850):

Topic: Is *Scarlet and Black* a story of success or failure?

Comment: An old but still quite reliable rule for the construction of a discussion or argument is that it should have three identifiable sections: an introduction; a development; and a conclusion.

This essay seems to me to have an approximation of those three parts. However, it is only the conclusion that is really recognisable as what it should be. And a conclusion that is preceded by a sketchy and unfocused introduction, and by a development that never comes to grips with the matter supposedly under discussion, can never be anything but a good intention.

Let your introduction be two things: a definition of terms; and a blueprint of the discussion to follow, the shape of the argument. In this topic, there are, it seems to me, two terms that should be clarified from the outset: success and failure. Each of these terms can bear at least two meanings: success and failure as judged by the world at large; and the same things as judged by the self. It is the paradox of this ambiguity that your introduction should have tried to clear up. In so doing, you would inevitably have had to pass on to your reader a hint about what shape your essay was going to take e.g. 'Having defined my terms as etc. etc., I now propose to examine the first of these terms etc. etc . . .' The reader would have had a clue about the trend of your argument before you get into it; and that is a great advantage to both you and your reader.

Your development: you have written a fairly thorough, very accurate, summary of the events that make up the plot of the novel. However, plot is not theme. And it is the theme of success/failure, as presented by Stendhal through the events, that you should have been examining.

It is obvious that you see the difference between Julien's public failure and private failure; but nowhere do you focus your mind on it and write the few paragraphs of discussion that it calls for. The theme is implicit in what you say and in the quotations which you choose from the text of the novel. But it should be explicit; otherwise there is no discussion of the evidence, merely the evidence presented as though it was self-explanatory.

A smaller point: when recounting plot, use the present tense; it is the usual thing. And pay attention to using the same tense all the time.

Notice my suggestion on page 3 about a better way to make sentences. If you write shorter sentences, if you teach yourself to pause and think of some other word every time you feel tempted to link clauses with *ands* and *buts*, then you will probably write more clearly and intelligently.

Notice, too, that some of your punctuation could improve.

Misspelling of proper names is a form of vermin; it should be stamped out by the simple device of checking them in the text.

As you can see from both sets of comments, the lecturer is conducting a discussion with the student, and there is an underlying assumption that the argument expressed in the essay is still open to further refinement and that the method of presentation can still be improved. These comments become part of the continuous process of learning; a further step, rather than a dead end.

3 Personal discussion: In some cases your lecturer may arrange to hand back your essay to you personally or ask you to come and discuss it individually at a later time. Although such an interview may seen daunting at first, it is often the most helpful form of feedback you can get. It gives you a chance to explain your ideas more thoroughly and to talk about more effective ways of presenting them. You can also ask your lecturer to explain in more detail the criticisms made of your essay.

Self-assessment

It is useful to judge your own essay on two grounds:

- what are the strengths and weaknesses of *what you did produce?*
- what are the strengths and weaknesses of *the way in which you worked* on the essay?

1 What did you produce? In judging your own work you will inevitably be influenced by the formal assessment you received. In fact you may find you disagree with some of the lecturer's criticisms even after you have considered them as objectively as you can. For example, the lecturer may have criticised your interpretation of a source or incident, but you may remain convinced that it does have the significance you have attributed to it. Well, there is no law that you must agree with everything your lecturer thinks. One lesson you might draw is that next time you must manage to present your views more convincingly.

It can be helpful to list separately, or highlight in different colours:

- the comments which bear on the *subject matter* of the essay—questions of fact, accuracy, evidence, sources, etc.
- the comments which bear on your *use* of your material—choice of quotations, analysis of different approaches, your conclusions, etc.
- the comments which bear on the *surface features* of your presentation—spelling, referencing format, etc.

You will then be in a position to plan your strategies for the writing of your next essay more clearly.

2 How did you work? In order to improve your working strategies, it might be helpful to ask yourself these questions:

- How efficient were my reading strategies:
    Did I spend too much time on general materials?
    Did I miss an important source?
- How useful were my notes:
    Did they cover much more material than I needed?
    Did they leave out essential details about sources?
    Were they easy to reorganise into a structure for the essay?
- Was the time I spent on thinking and planning well spent:
    Should I have spent more or less time on this stage?
    How representative of the final essay was my original outline plan?
- Did I start the writing stage too soon, or too late?
- Are there ways I might have cut down on the redrafting and editing stages, or should I have allowed more time for these?

Discussion with other students

A final, and often neglected, strategy is to discuss your work with fellow students. If you can persuade a small group of friends to swap essays which have been marked and graded, this is a most useful pooling of resources. It may be a difficult procedure to get started, but it can help you to understand the qualities of thinking and writing which constitute a good essay and the variety of ways in which the same task can be tackled.

Summary

In this short chapter we have suggested that the assessment of your completed essay is an essential stage in the continuous process of learning. Through analysing the response of your lecturer to your essay, through evaluating your own methods of writing, and by comparing your essay and ideas with those of other students, you can improve your future performance.

The main points to remember are:

1 It is important to understand why your lecturer commented upon and graded your essay as he or she did.
2 Discussion of your work with your lecturer and with other students is often the most useful source of feedback.

Chapter 10

Writing reviews and reports

So far we have talked about writing essays—the most common type of written assignment that you will meet in your courses. But you may also encounter some more specialised types of assignment such as book reviews and research reports which present demands additional to those we have discussed already. Some requirements remain constant, of course, no matter whether you are writing essays, reviews or reports. In all cases, for example, you are expected to think critically about your content. Similarly, you must still analyse and present that content in such a way that your reader is persuaded of the force of your conclusion or evaluation. But your lecturers will have particular expectations about the style and format of reviews and reports, and you will need to be aware of the nature of these expectations.

Here we will look very briefly at three special types of assignments:

1 the book review;
2 the research lab report; and
3 the fieldwork report.

1 Book review

In later year courses you may be asked to write a book review; often this is the first written assignment set in a course. A close and critical reading of a book provides a good introduction to a new topic or to the theoretical base of the discipline or to the current state of knowledge in the field. The purpose of such a review is not, as in reviews in newspapers, merely to highlight the key features of the book in such a way that your reader will be encouraged to rush off and buy it for Christmas. Here your review is being written for a reader (your lecturer) who is already knowledgeable in the discipline. Your lecturer is not so much interested in whether you can summarise the content of the book as in whether you can critically assess the quality of the ideas, the data and the arguments being presented by the author.

In most cases your review will have to answer some or all of the following questions:

• Is this an important book (within the discipline)? Why? or why not?
• What range of material does it cover?
• What theoretical approach is used in presenting this material?
• What are the particular strengths and weaknesses of the author's discussion?
• What is your overall evaluation of this book, and for what reasons?

If you turn to Appendix 10, you will find examples of book review assignments from two different disciplines which indicate the specific purposes the lecturers had in mind when they set these tasks.

Writing the review

Step 1 Get a feel of the book you have selected to review by using your skimming skills.

• Glance at the title, table of contents, and the Preface or Introduction. These should give you some idea of the coverage of the book and its method of organisation and, if the Preface is useful, also the author's reason for writing.
• Skim quickly through the whole book, running your eye over headings and sub-headings and over opening sentences of paragraphs. Look quickly at any tables, illustrations or other graphic materials. This should confirm and extend your initial impression of the scope and focus of the author's work.
• Read more closely the first chapter. This will usually set out the main issues to be discussed and indicate the theoretical or conceptual framework within which the author proposes to work.

- Read closely the final chapter, which should cover the author's conclusions and summarise the main reasons why these conclusions have been reached.

Step 2 Now you must go back and read the book in more detail, and decide which aspects you wish to discuss in your review. Maybe you think the most important part is the theoretical approach, or the data presented, or a particular case study used, or the author's selection and interpretation of evidence, or the range of coverage, or the style of presentation. At this stage you will be taking notes, identifying key quotations and so gathering your own data from your source. Nearly always you will choose to discuss the issues the author has identified as being important, but sometimes you may want to concentrate on a relatively minor point in the book because it is a central point in the course you are studying. In any case you are beginning to shape your own review by the decisions you make at this stage.

Step 3 Depending on the length of your review, you may want to read other articles or chapters of books to find supporting evidence or different models or alternative interpretations of data to those presented by your author. You may also want to glance at (but not reproduce) reviews of the book in recent academic journals. Apart from providing you with a model for academic book reviews, this additional reading will give you some feel for the way the book has been received within the discipline. In this way you will become better informed about the general field of study and more confident in your own evaluation of the particular work you are reviewing.

Step 4 You are now ready to start drafting your assignment. The structure of the review should include:

- an *initial identification* of the book (author, date, title, publisher) and an indication of the major aspects of the book you will be discussing;
- a *brief summary* of the range, contents and argument of the book. Occasionally you may need to summarise chapter by chapter but in a short review you usually pick out the main themes only. Here you also point out the theoretical perspective or viewpoint from which the book is written. (This section would normally take up about a third of your total review);
- a *critical discussion* of two to three key issues raised in the book. This section is the core of your review. You need to make clear the author's own argument and evidence before you criticise and evaluate it. And

you must support your criticisms with evidence from the text or from other writings. You may want to indicate gaps in the author's treatment of a topic, but it is seldom useful to criticise writers for not doing something they never intended or claimed to do; and

- a *final evaluation* of the overall contribution this book has made to your understanding of the topic (and, maybe, its importance to the development of the discipline, setting it in the context of other writings in the field).

Appendix 10 also includes a brief checklist which you may find useful when you are writing the final draft of your review.

2 Research lab report

In many science courses you are required to write regular lab reports which follow a format set out in your lab manual and are very similar to those you learned to write in school. However in some courses, such as psychology, you may be asked to write a lab report which is, in fact, much more like an article in an academic journal—indeed the prescribed format is often copied from a leading journal in the discipline. This can be a tricky task until you become familiar with the style and format that are expected.

In Appendix 12 we refer to a book on scientific writing by David Lindsay which you may find helpful when writing such reports.

Your report will normally be divided into four sections (together with a Bibliography or list of References you have cited in your report, and maybe some Appendices for additional data):

1 Introduction: Here you justify the need for, and design of, your research project. You have to show how it fits into the main field of inquiry and how it derives from previous research. The normal way to do this is to refer to the major research studies which are relevant to your investigation (in longer reports this is commonly known as a literature review). You will have to discuss the links and the gaps in the previous research in order to show the intention underlying your own study or experiment. Is it merely replicating someone else's study to verify their results? Or is it actually intended to clarify a problem that your discussion of previous research has highlighted? Maybe it is designed to fill some gap in the research record, or to take the research one step further? This underlying intention must then be made clear in the final paragraph of your Introduction where you set out, in very concise form, the aims or hypotheses of your project.

2 Materials and methods: In this section you set out all the details of your sample, your research design and methodology, and the instruments you used in your study. The information you provide should be detailed enough to allow your reader to follow or repeat your experiment.

3 Results: Here you present the results of your investigation in quantitative form, usually in tables and usually with statistical applications. Each table must be clearly headed with all the relevant information about subjects and scales of measurement necessary for a full interpretation of the data. You usually have to summarise the main points of each table in words, drawing attention to any significant findings. Such findings become the subject of discussion in the final section of your report. If you are asked to submit all your raw data (i.e. before they have been categorised into separate tables or submitted to statistical analysis), you can do this in an Appendix to the report.

4 Discussion: You should start this section by immediately showing the relationship of your findings to your original aims or hypotheses, as stated at the end of your Introduction. You need then to discuss the significance of your findings and comment on unexpected variations or contradictions in your results. In doing this you will probably find yourself drawing on some of the studies you referred to in your introduction. It is common to conclude a report by suggesting improvements or variations that should be made in any further research on this topic.

Normally in lab reports students are told to avoid the use of personal pronouns ('Don't use I'), but more and more lecturers are now not only permitting but actually encouraging such usage—mostly on the grounds that it asserts a degree of personal responsibility for the claims made in the report. If in doubt about this, ask your lecturer.

In Appendix 11 you will find a convenient checklist against which you can assess the final draft of your lab report before you submit it.

3 Fieldwork report

In some courses, maybe geography, environmental studies, or sociology, you might be asked to do some fieldwork and then write it up in the form of a report. Depending on the course, you may have to record data collected via a survey or some other form of measurement. This material then becomes the basis of your report, and your main task is two-fold: you have to present the data you have collected; and you must offer some interpretation of its significance.

Fieldwork reports tend to be more flexible and varied in structure than the tightly controlled lab report described above. Nevertheless the fieldwork report is a variant on the lab report rather than a totally separate species of writing, and you will usually find that such reports have a common underlying structure:

Title
Introduction (including aim)
Methods (where applicable)
Presentation of data
Discussion
Conclusion
Bibliography or References
Appendices (where applicable).

Normally your lecturer will provide guidelines on matters of structure and format: you may, for example, be asked to provide an Abstract in addition to what is laid out above or, if your report is very long, a table of contents.

Apart from the general headings suggested above, fieldwork reports tend to make frequent use of sub-headings and sub-divisions, and the data are often presented in graphic or tabular form, either in the body of the report or in Appendices. The guiding principle for these reports is that you are looking for a structure and format which will allow you to present your information, and the interpretation of that information, as clearly as possible to your reader.

Summary

In this chapter we have looked at some writing tasks which have very specific requirements in terms of structure and format: the book review, the research lab report, and the fieldwork report. They all require critical and analytical thought, and the logical development of an argument or point of view is still basic to such assignments though less obvious than in a conventional essay.

The main points to remember are:

1 It is important to follow the guidelines set out by your lecturer or modelled in the relevant academic journal.
2 Your writing should focus on your data, whether in the form of a book or research findings, and you must draw your conclusions largely from that material.

Chapter 11

Exam essays

So, you've learnt to write essays. You've learnt to spend time analysing an essay topic, reading around the subject, gradually working your way into an understanding of what is required, redrafting your initial writing, clarifying your ideas and argument.

But you will need to change some of these methods of working if you are to handle exam essays competently.

Change what? The way in which you prepare. The speed at which you work. Your ways of actually planning and writing an exam answer. In the exam room, limited time and lack of source materials will force you to make these changes to your pattern of working. Nonetheless, you will find that those skills and habits which you have already developed in writing term essays are also important for exam essays. The whole process of essay writing will be speeded up, but the intellectual tasks are similar.

Your efficiency in an exam will depend to a great extent on the effectiveness of your preparation. And a good way to start your revision is to think about the differing expectations of your lecturers about exam essays in contrast to term essays.

Expectations

Lecturers' expectations about term essays (see Chapter 1)	Lecturers' expectations about exam essays
1 It is expected that your essay will be clearly focused on the set topic and will deal fully with its central concerns (p. 4).	1 The same, except 'deal fully' will imply 'as fully as possible within the limits of the exam time'.
2 It is expected that your essay will be the result of wide and critical reading (p. 6).	2 Your essay will be the result of systematic revision of the materials used in the course.
3 It is expected that your essay will present a reasoned argument (p. 8).	3 The same, though your exam essay is not expected to be as well–structured because there is little time for redrafting.
4 It is expected that your essay will be competently presented (p. 9).	4 Less important, except possibly the legibility of your handwriting.

Identifying probable exam topics

How can you set about revising effectively when you don't know what the exam will be about? It's certainly a problem, but there are ways in which you can start to identify the topics which will *probably* be set. You can never be certain that a particular topic will turn up, and you will have almost no clues as to the precise wording and focus of the actual questions on the paper. However, you can narrow the range of topics with some confidence.

Here are three ways in which you might start this process:

1 Look at past exam papers. These are useful, but never sure, guides. There may have been a change of lecturer, or of some of the course content, or of the style and format of the exam (for example, a shift from three essays to three short answers and a multiple-choice section).

Initially your purpose in skimming past exam papers is to:

- *identify the main topics* which are covered. For example, is there usually a question on kinship in the anthropology exam? Or on meteorology in the geography paper?
- become familiar with the *format* of the exam. For example, how many questions are set, and within what time limits? Is the paper divided into sections? Are any sections compulsory?

2 Use any departmental sources which you can find to clarify your understanding of the content of the course and, therefore, of the probable scope of the exam paper. Departmental handouts and the course outline in the Faculty Handbook should give you a brief summary of the aims and content of the course. This can help you to identify both the key concepts and issues which have been covered during the semester or year and the rationale underlying the whole course.

3 Read through all your lecture notes and tutorial notes, both to refresh your memory of the whole sweep of the course and to identify the main divisions into which the course falls.

Now you should be in a position to pick out the specific topics you want to concentrate on in your revision.

Reading and other revision activities

In your reading for a term essay you are trying to find relevant sources and extend your understanding of the topic. In revising for exams, by contrast, you are trying to consolidate and clarify the knowledge you have already acquired. So your study strategies must change. Revision must be an active process in which you rework and rethink your materials in a variety of ways.

Here are some suggestions:

1 Make *summaries* of your notes as you read and try to *condense* a whole section of the course into a page or two of notes. In this way you are forcing yourself to identify key points. These points, recombined in new ways to meet the specific demands of your exam questions, will be as much material as you can handle in the exam time. These summaries also have the advantage that they can be used effectively in the final stages of your revision when you are desperately trying to remind yourself of everything you should already know. They can give you confidence that the task is manageable.

2 Check your revision notes against *past exam papers*:

- which questions relate to the material you have been revising?
- what points would you need to cover in order to answer each question?

3 You can also try framing *your own exam questions* based on the materials you are revising.

(These three strategies are particularly valuable if you are working in a study group. The comments, insights and different approaches of other students can help to sharpen your own ideas.)

4 You may also find it useful to write a *trial answer* to one question, without looking at your revision notes and within the time limit of the exam. Some lecturers and tutors are willing to skim through these trial efforts and comment on your performance. Other students may be helpful in suggesting ways in which you could have handled the topic more effectively. And even if you can get no outside feedback, this exercise is still useful in demonstrating just how much—or how little—you can write on a question within the limited time.

5 In some courses you may be allowed to take notes and other materials into the exam room. However, you'll need to *organise* these materials beforehand so that you can use them quickly and efficiently within the exam time limits.

Planning and writing

Exams demand a quick response; but also a response that is accurately directed to the terms of the set question. You may find it helpful to keep these three steps in mind as you start your actual exam:

1 Once you have chosen the questions you will answer, make notes for each (on the exam paper, on rough paper, anywhere) on the points, facts, names, dates and other relevant information which immediately come to mind. Later these first responses must be reorganised coherently, but they can be very helpful both in starting your mind working and in assisting you to switch your concentration to the next question as soon as you have completed one answer.

2 Before you start planning each answer, look closely at the wording of the question. Make quite sure that you have understood the content you must cover and the way in which you are directed to use it.

3 Plan your answer as clearly as possible *before* you start writing.

By comparison with term essay writing, the exam allows you the opportunity for *only one draft*. Inevitably this will result in a rougher presentation: there may be awkward links between one point and the next; the direction of your argument may shift; you may remember points late in your essay which should have appeared earlier; the introduction and conclusion may not be very polished. If you are used to writing your essays on a computer you may find that, without practice in the period leading up to exams, you may get writer's cramp when you suddenly switch to handwriting under time pressures. To some extent your examiner will make allowances for these shortcomings. On the other hand, those exam answers which exhibit the qualities of a good essay will be appreciated.

Editing

Editing (if it takes place at all) is a very hasty process in exams. It is commonplace advice that you allow five minutes (or more) at the end of each exam answer for editing. In practice, if you do have time to spare, certainly go back over your answers to correct errors of fact, style and grammar. However, in many exams you will find you have little time, or taste, for rereading what you have written. You must rely on the fluent style and the habits of accuracy and clarity which you have been consciously developing over the year's work.

Summary

In this final chapter we have discussed some of the adaptations you must make to your essay writing methods when you are handling exam essays. The most significant differences arise from the constraints on time and access to source materials. Efficient revision is the basis for effective exam answers.

The main points to remember are:

1 In your exam essays you should aim for the same qualities as in your term essays, though your answers will probably be less competently argued and less polished.
2 You should begin your revision by trying to identify the topics on which exam questions will probably be based.
3 Good revision is an active process in which you rework your material so that it can be used with flexibility and efficiency in the exam.
4 Working in a study group is a particularly useful strategy for revision.
5 In the exam you should analyse and plan each answer clearly before you start writing it.
6 Your approach to exam essays and your success in handling them will reflect the competence you have developed in essay writing throughout the whole course.

Appendices

Further practice and examples

Appendix 1   Practice in analysing a reading list
Appendix 2   Practice in skimming for understanding
Appendix 3   Practice in skimming for an essay topic
Appendix 4   Modifications of skimming: an example
Appendix 5   Essay plans: examples
Appendix 6   Reorganisation of the first draft: an example
Appendix 7   Introductions: further examples
Appendix 8   Introduction: process of redrafting
Appendix 9   Features of academic style: an example
Appendix 10   Writing a book review
Appendix 11   Checklist for a psychology lab report

Information

Appendix 12   Suggested reference books and supplementary
              materials
Appendix 13   Direct quotations
Appendix 14   References
Appendix 15   Bibliography

Appendix  7

Practice in analysing a reading list (see Chapter 3)

Look at the following topic and related reading list which were given to students in a prehistory course. Following the suggestions made in Chapter 3, analyse the list in relation to the set topic in order to decide:

- what you can learn from the reading list about the content and tasks involved in the essay;
- which might be the best books or articles to read initially.

You might also consider why the lecturer has recommended an article written in 1890, and why an article on an orangutan might be relevant to the essay topic.

Topic: What can we learn from experimental replication of stone artefacts?

Reading list:

Binford, S.R. & L.R. (1969), 'Stone tools and human behaviour', *Scientific American*, **220**, no. 4, pp. 70–84.

Coles, J.M. (1973), *Archaeology by Experiment*, Hutchinson.

Crabtree, D. (1972), 'An introduction to flintworking', *Occ. Papers of Idaho State Museum*, no. 28.

Gibson, K. & Ingold, T. (eds) (1993), *Tools, Language and Cognition in Human Evolution*, CUP.

Holmes, W.H. (1890), 'A quarry workshop of the flaked-stone implement makers in the District of Columbia', *American Anthropologist*, **3**, pp. 1–26.

Schick, K. & Toth, N. (1993), *Making Silent Stones Speak*, Simon & Schuster.

Semenov, S.A. (1964), *Prehistoric Technology*, Cory, Adams & Mackay.

Wright, R.V.S. (1972), 'Imitative learning of a flaked stone technology—The case of an orangutan', *Mankind*, **8**, pp. 296–306.

Appendix  2

Practice in skimming for understanding (see Chapter 3)

Step 1: Skim section III of the Blainey chapter by reading only the first sentences of each paragraph.

Step 2: Here are the sentences you have just read quickly:

The Australian trade, about which most is known, linked coastal and inland areas in Arnhem Land.

He found that each area specialized in producing certain goods and in receiving others.

'Each individual in Arnhem Land', wrote Donald Thomson, 'is the centre of a great ceremonial exchange cycle'.

On the Daly River, about 400 miles to the west, a similar commerce between tribes and within tribes had been observed even earlier by another gifted anthropologist, W.E.H. Stanner.

There are several puzzles about the exchange of goods in northern Australia.

Such a sharp distinction between the social and the economic, between ceremonial exchange and economic exchange, is perhaps invalid.

Reading between the lines of the fascinating evidence which Donald Thomson set out in his small red book we begin to see that it was much closer to barter and trade than he realized.

When aboriginal commerce is dissected it no longer appears so different from modern commerce.

The exchange of goods in several near-coastal regions of the Northern Territory was not only trade but a vital expression of social solidarity.

The social and economic were lock and key.

Step 3: Even if some of these sentences are not fully clear to you (for example, who is 'he' in the second sentence?), can you still begin to understand the content and the argument of this section?

Step 4: Now read the whole section in full, noting how long this takes you.

Step 5: Consider the advantages you gained from the full reading (more information; a fuller understanding of the passage) and weigh these against the advantages of your previous skimming.

There is no 'right' conclusion to be reached—the point is to recognise the advantages and limitations of skimming so that you can make use of this skill when you think it is appropriate.

Appendix  3

Practice in skimming for an essay topic (see Chapter 3)

1 Assume that you have been set the essay topic:

How far was the movement of goods in Aboriginal society a matter of ritual exchange and how far was it based on economic motives?

2 Skim the whole Blainey extract in order to identify the material you think will be relevant to this topic.

3 Think over the following questions:

- How long, approximately, has this taken you?
- Which parts of the chapter would you need to reread more fully?
- If you compare the sections of the chapter which are relevant for this essay topic with the sections which were important for the essay you worked on in Chapter 3 (p. 34), what can you deduce about the content and task of each essay?
- Can you identify areas which you would need to cover in this essay which are not covered in the Blainey chapter?
- Would you organise your essay in the same way that Blainey has presented his material in this chapter?

Appendix 4

Modifications of skimming: an example (see Chapter 3)

Look at the following extract from a psychology text and try skimming in the normal fashion, by reading *only* the first sentences of each paragraph.

I.Q. and age

As has been said, the ability to pass increasingly difficult items on intelligence tests grows rapidly during the years from birth to about the mid-teens—and particularly in the earliest years of childhood. This fact leads to some interesting questions: At what age does the kind of ability measured by intelligence tests reach its peak? Once the peak is attained, does the ability then decline during middle and old age?

The answers to these questions are not easy to obtain, because they are complicated by the probability, which has just been mentioned, that the average score on intelligence tests has been rising generation by generation in recent years. If one were to administer the same kind of intelligence test to large numbers of people from teenagers to sixty-year-olds, one would naturally expect the younger people to make higher average scores than the older people—and this is indeed what has been found to happen.

For example, in standardizing a recent version of the Wechsler Adult Intelligence Scale, the test was administered to representative samples of various age groups from sixteen through sixty-four, and the results were as illustrated in graph 1. Note that the average total score rose through the early twenties, remained more or less on a plateau until thirty-four, then began a fairly sharp and steady decline. However, the age-by-age patterns differed for the two parts of the test, the verbal items and the performance items. Ability at verbal skills, after reaching its peak between twenty-five and thirty-four, remained fairly constant through the age of forty-four and afterward showed only a relatively small decline. Ability on performance ¬s began to decline after the early twenties and at a fairly rapid rate.

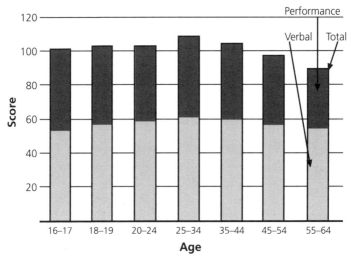

Graph 1 I.Q. by age groups. Various age groups make different scores on the Wechsler Adult Intelligence Scale; the differences are apparent in both the verbal and performance parts of the test and in the total score as well. For a discussion of these results, see the text.

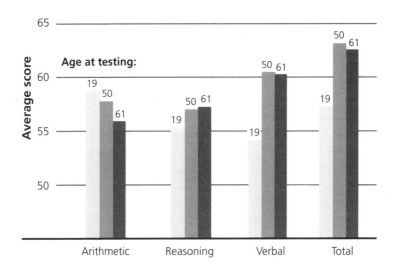

Graph 2 At what age are we smartest? The bars show the scores (not I.Q.'s) for three of the skills measured by an intelligence test, as well as the total score, made by men who were first tested when they were nineteen-year-old college freshmen, again when they were fifty, and a third time when they were sixty-one.

What would be the results of a study in which the very same people could be tested over the years, beginning in their teens and continuing into their sixties? Despite the difficulties of making such a study, fortunately one investigator has managed to compare the scores made on a group intelligence test by nearly a hundred men during the First World War, when they were college freshmen averaging nineteen years old, with their scores on the same kind of test taken when they were fifty years old and again when they were sixty-one. The results are illustrated in graph 2.

As the figure shows, scores on the arithmetic items in the test were highest at the age of nineteen and went down steadily thereafter. Scores on items measuring reasoning ability did just the opposite; they rose steadily and were highest at sixty-one. Scores on items measuring verbal ability were substantially higher at fifty than at nineteen but then declined slightly at sixty-one. The total score rose markedly from nineteen to fifty and afterward showed a slight decline. The results are not entirely satisfactory because they are for men only—and for a group that had an above-average I.Q. at first testing and presumably led lives more favourable than average to continued intellectual growth. However, they do offer a strong indication that intelligence—at least as measured by present tests—is by no means the monopoly of the young and that there is hardly any cause for despair over what will happen to our mental abilities as we get older.

from J. Kagan & E. Havemann (1976), *Psychology: An Introduction*, Harcourt, Brace, Jovanovich, Inc., New York, pp. 432-434.

You probably have found that skimming this passage by opening sentences does not yield any sensible structure. For example, the opening sentence of the second paragraph ('The answers to these questions are not easy to obtain . . .') can only be understood if you look back to the 'questions' which occur at the end of the previous paragraph. Similarly, the clue to the meaning of the first sentence in paragraph 5 ('As the figure shows . . .') lies in the final sentence of the fourth paragraph. However, once you have recognised the way in which the argument is organised, you can adapt your skimming procedure to take advantage of the structure; in this example you would probably skim both the first *and* final sentences of each paragraph. Similarly, if a writer tends to use the first sentences as bridges, then you would focus quickly on the two opening sentences of each paragraph.

Appendix  5

Essay plans: example (see Chapter 6)

Here are plans developed by three students in a first-year geography course. The students were required to write a 1500 word essay on the following topic:

> 'Urban planning in Britain since 1940 has improved the nature of cities in that country.'
>
> Discuss this statement with particular reference to the planning of London.

All three used the same four books as sources:

> R. Goodman, *After the Planners*, Penguin, 1972.
> P. Hall, *The World Cities*, World Univ. Library, 1966.
> — *Urban and Regional Planning*, Penguin, 1977 (rev. edn).
> H. Stretton, *Urban Planning in Rich and Poor Countries*, OUP, 1978.

On the basis of their reading and what they learnt in lectures, they all reached the same general conclusion:

> Yes, urban planning has improved the structure of London; but its effect on the quality of life and social objectives in the city is less certain.

The essay plans they produced, however, were very different. Anna, the student in Chapter 6 who claimed she tries to 'block out on a piece of paper the main points I want to make' and also notes likely quotes and references, produced the following outline:

'Urban planning in Britain, since 1940, has improved how far??
define the nature of cities? in that country.' Discuss — re.
planning of London.

* Intro — Stretton quote re 'complicated' mod. city (p.10)
  — re London (nb. main Reports) → struct change /
     urban   also 'nature'?
Style of planning
     Gout > private enterprise (Goodman)
        — '40 Barlow, '44 Aberc., '47 S.E.System
     Green belt → New Towns / 'home & neighbourhood'
                                        (Stret. p 104)

Nature of cities / London
     ① Pop. density
     ② Services
     ③ industry   get stats / tables
                               from Hall (p. 54)

Nb white collar employ

Plans — slums / decentralize / but concent.
        — Commuter belt   services in L.

RESULTS 1. old problems transf. to NTs
         dev. etc.   } new
         2. quality of life — transport, } problems
                        pollution

Concl. Yes, but no !!!

Ben, on the other hand, who explained his method of developing a series of increasingly detailed outlines, produced this highly systematic plan:

'Urban planning in Britain since 1940 has improved the nature of cities in that country.' Discuss this statement with particular reference to the planning of London.

Introduction: Structure of cities improved significantly — but not social planning/quality of life/welfare.

1. Brief background: pressures for planning and change
   — postwar baby boom: 66mil. by end of century
   — pop. segmenting into smaller and smaller households
   — increasing mobility
   — inter-regional migration to London and South
   — rising prosperity, eg cars, bigger houses (Hall 156ft.)

2. Changes in structure (focus on London)
   (a) Legislation - 1945   Abercrombie's Greater London P. (based Barlow '40) → 30 miles London ring, decentralisation, 5 mile Green Belt, 1m to be housed in overspill New Towns
   —plus distribution of Industry Act (many loopholes) → 1947 Town and Country Planning Act: limited dev. of inner London — 'nationalised right to develop land' (Hall)
   1949 National Parks and Access to Countryside Act: rec. areas and rights of public to countryside

   (b) Extent of change
   i) Migration: 1949–50 — 14 NTs (Eng and Wales) and London overspills
   By 1971 — 29 NTs, pop of 1m
   but   inter-regional mig. to L and South till 1966

   ii) Reconstruction: 1950s major slum clearance and reconstruction programs (inc. high-rise) ← shortage of land

   iii) Transport: 1950s — L 'worst congested' (Hall) road system in world — commuting from NTs → motorways, multi-storey carparks.

BUT 3. Neglect of social objectives and quality fo life
   (a) high rise dev./displacement of low income from housing with no adequate replacement. Urban decay. High income to peripheral suburbs
   (b) quality of services (education, transport) and physical environ. (air, water) deteriorating in inner urban areas
   (c) employment: dislocation?

Conclusion: Improvement at macro level in physical structure but need to plan for social objectives only realised with hindsight.

A third student, Edward, produced a quite different approach:

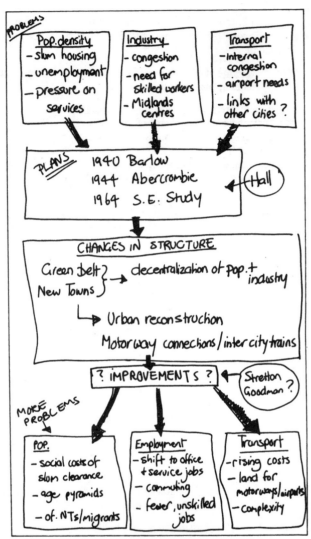

If you compare these plans for the same essay, you may find that one system appeals more strongly to your own style of working. Or that you have developed an individual system of planning which suits you. You may even agree with David, the student in Chapter 6, who starts writing in order to clarify his argument. Whatever the case, the important point is that there is no one way that suits everyone and that is clearly superior on all occasions.

All of these students were awarded Credits for the essays they finally wrote.

Appendix  6.

Reorganisation of the first draft: an example (see Chapter 7)

Here are the stages a student went through in reorganising a first–year sociology essay.

> **Topic:** Drawing on personal experience of ceremonies (marriage, funerals, graduations, prize-giving, etc.), discuss the extent to which Garfinkel's criteria apply to all ceremonies involving status alteration. (*Text:* H. Garfinkel, 'Conditions of successful degradation ceremonies'.)

First draft: 'Conditions of successful degradation ceremonies', an article by Harold Garfinkel, indicates a specific form of the rites of passage; that is a manner through which an individual undergoes a change in status using a ceremony to mark the occasion. Garfinkel's criteria apply to some changes of status whether positive or negative but cannot be used to describe all status changes.

Garfinkel's article states that the degradation ceremony is made up of several points. The first is the ritual separation and ostracising of the individual (known as the perpetrator), the second is the ceremony in which he (the perpetrator) has status removed (in front of witnesses) and emerges a degraded individual.

A most notable degradation ceremony (and one to which Garfinkel's ideas can be applied) occurs when an army officer is publicly stripped of his commission. The officer is set apart from his peers, ostracised and noted as a deviant from army norms. He is then taken to a ceremony presided over by a notable army personage (in whom the army vests its authority); during this ceremony, the officer is stripped of his rank. *However,* another more common occurrence of degradation which cannot be applied to Garfinkel's criteria is that of an unwed mother. Society denounces an unwed mother and ostracises her throughout her pregnancy but doesn't set her apart from society though a stigma is attached to the child's illegitimacy. There is no ceremony to mark this change of status but society sees the mother's actions as a threat to its codes.

Some positive changes in status conform to Garfinkel's criteria; one of these is Christian marriage. The wedding date is announced and the couple involved are ritually separated from society and each other and are brought together in the church. The bride walks down the aisle on her father's left— an inferior position—the couple is separated from the congregation (witnesses) and from the priest who officiates at the wedding. The priest is recognised as an upholder of Christian society's morals. The man and the woman are ceremonially united as one entity and they both emerge married and the woman (generally) takes the husband's name. Another status change which conforms to Garfinkel's ideas is that of a graduation ceremony. The student is also set aside from society and walks down a corridor to the ceremony. The ceremony (at university graduations) is conducted by the Vice-Chancellor. He confers the degree on the student in front of many witnesses and the student then emerges with a degree. *But Garfinkel's criteria do not wholly apply to a coming-out ceremony in the Trobriand Islands.* The ceremony occurs three months after childbirth when a mother who has been segregated from the rest of the village comes back into society. The ceremony is only celebrated by the family and a few close friends with no apparent master or mistress of ceremonies. The mother comes out dressed in traditional garb with betelnut makeup and a head-dress to denote the occasion. The woman then assumes the role of motherhood and increased status involved with childbirth.

Garfinkel's article stating the events of degradation can also be applied to gradation ceremonies. However, its use is limited as many gradation and degradation ceremonies do not follow the same format.

As it stands, the flow of thought is somewhat difficult to follow. This is because the paragraphing is haphazard. Remember those general insights about the paragraph we discussed in Chapter 3? That the paragraph is the basic unit of thought? That statements within one paragraph should cohere around one basic idea? That it is often a useful technique to lead with the main idea at the head of the paragraph? Now look at the organisation of paragraphs in this first draft:

Paragraph 1: Explanation of Garfinkel's theory of degradation ceremonies, and the qualification that the term cannot be used to describe all status changes.

Paragraph 2: Analysis of the structure of a degradation ceremony. Examples: (1) demotion of an army officer—meets Garfinkel's criteria.

Paragraph 3: *However* (2) society's treatment of an unwed mother—
does not meet criteria.

Paragraph 4: Examples: (3) marriage and (4) graduation are positive
examples of status change ceremonies—these meet
Garfinkel's criteria.
But (5) criteria only partly applicable to a Trobriand
coming-out ceremony.

Paragraph 5: Garfinkel's criteria cannot be applied to all ceremonies
involving status alteration.

In this draft the student had attempted to get down in words both
a summary of the basic concept being examined and a variety of
examples to which this concept could be applied. But how far is the
present arrangement of material in paragraph units effective? What is
the effect on the reader of the two longer paragraphs in the middle of
the essay by comparison with the much shorter ones at the beginning
and end? Are the examples arranged in the order which most effectively
develops the argument that Garfinkel's criteria are not universally
applicable? Are there significant shifts in the thinking in paras 3 and
4, indicated by the contrast-setting terms *however* and *but*? (These
words were not in italics in the original draft).

This student, following a group discussion, revised her essay according to the following structure:

Paragraph 1: A combination of the original paragraphs 1 and 2,
focused on Garfinkel's theory and criteria.

Paragraph 2: Analysis of examples 1, 3 and 4 which all meet
Garfinkel's criteria and which include both positive and
negative changes in status.

Paragraph 3: Analysis of examples 2 and 5 which do not meet all the
criteria and are examples of contrasting change in status
following childbirth.

Paragraph 4: Conclusion.

She still had to do more revision on the actual wording and style of
the essay and to clarify the opening sentences of each paragraph. In
general, however, the restructuring of the material at the paragraph
level was the major achievement of the redrafting stage. The essay is
now more logically structured and better balanced.

Appendix  7

Introductions: further examples (see Chapter 7)

Here are two introductions to the same essay topic in an English literature course.

> **Topic:** A novelist has many possible ways of letting the reader know what a character is 'like': straight-forward narrative commentary, for example, or first-person narration in which the character tells his or her thoughts, concerns, feelings. In most familiar forms of drama, however, a character must be portrayed only externally and indirectly through dialogue, appearance and action. Discuss Ibsen's characterisation of Hedda Gabler, paying particular attention to specific ways in which he attempts to show the audience what sort of a person Hedda is.

Example 1

In *Hedda Gabler* Hedda is portrayed by Ibsen externally and indirectly. Hedda's mind is not deeply explored by Ibsen, so that we, the audience, are invited to reconstruct her character from her utterances, her situation and her actions. Specifically, Ibsen attempts to show the audience Hedda's character through comments on her by other characters and by Hedda's conversations with the others. One can also learn about Hedda's character through her reactions to her present situation and her attachment to her past.

Example 2

Hedda Gabler is a play with a central personality initiating the action, and seemingly in control. Hedda, the central character, sets up the action; for example, she is the one to get Tesman to write to Lovborg (p. 282), giving her the opportunity to cross-examine Mrs Elvsted. Hedda is also the instigator in Lovborg's demise of character and his subsequent death (p. 308).

Example 1 sets out systematically both the writer's point of view about the topic (Hedda is presented 'externally and indirectly') and the areas through which the writer will move in order to establish the validity of that point of view. Though the paragraph is far from perfect in style, the writer has achieved her purpose.

Now look again at the topic and Example 2. Is Example 2 an effective opening? Is it well focused on the topic? On the basis of those two openings, which essay seems more likely to meet the demands of the topic?

Appendix  8

Introduction: process of redrafting (see Chapter 7)

Here are three stages one student went through in trying to clarify the ideas in her introduction.

Topic: How effective a President was George Washington? What were his main contributions to the office of the Presidency? What was his view of the Constitution?

1st attempt

George Washington was not a terribly brilliant man but was extremely ambitious. In his younger years, Washington was a grand manager of his own affairs and that of the first government of America.

His ambition in early life led him to be an officer in the Royal Army against the French. During the War of Independence he became America's 'nation-wide' hero after bringing the 'Yankees' to victory.

2nd attempt

Within the framework of the Constitution, George Washington created the role of the President of the United States of America. Washington's effectiveness as a president rested upon his views and interpretation of the constitution. The office of the President was expressed on paper as an executive power, a commander in chief of the Army, Navy, and militia of the states as well as a treaty maker and an overall administrator. George Washington was not merely effective in carrying out these powers, but he gave the office importance and dignity which has since been associated with the U.S. Presidency . . .

(This draft continued without any paragraph breaks for two pages, as the student was primarily concerned at this stage with clarifying her ideas.)

3rd attempt

Within the framework of the Constitution of 1787, George Washington created the role of the President. Overall, Washington's effectiveness rested upon his activities as President which were modified by his views and interpretation of the Constitution. The President was defined by the Constitution as a holder of executive power, a commander-in-chief of the Army, Navy and militia of the states as well as a treaty maker and an administrator. George Washington was not merely effective in carrying out these duties but he gave the office the dignity and importance which have since been associated with the U.S. Presidency.

If you compare these three versions you may recognise the shifts through which this student's thinking has gone. Her first version is purely descriptive detail about George Washington and would be a poor introduction to an analytical essay. Her second version moves much more directly into analysing and pulling together the main strands of the set topic though, as yet, it has no clear shape. The third version, which could still be improved in style, is a much clearer attempt to place the significance of George Washington's contribution to the Presidency within an analytical framework which can be worked out in detail in the body of the essay.

Appendix 9

Features of academic style: an example (see Chapter 7)

Check if you can identify some of those features of academic style we discussed on p. 76–77. Read the following extract from a sociology textbook in order to find answers to these questions:

- what sort of *approach* does the writer use?
- how would you describe the *tone* of this extract?
- can you pick out any of the features of *grammar and vocabulary* we listed on p. 77?

To get you started, let's examine the first sentence of the extract. What characteristic features of academic style can you notice?

Are not both psychology and sociology, then, it might be asked, equally concerned with the way individual behaviour is socially conditioned?

approach	—a tentative debate, an invitation to more precise exploration, an appeal to reason.
tone	—formal language (how would you ask this question in ordinary speech?), impersonal, a 'lofty' rhetorical question.
grammar & vocabulary	—the clause 'it might be asked' is introduced by an *impersonal pronoun* (it) and uses a *passive* form of the verb (be asked); see too the verb 'is conditioned'.
	—the use of this secondary clause makes the sentence structure *complex*.
	—the word 'conditioned' is used in a more *specialised* sense here than in ordinary speech.

Read on now for yourself, trying as you go to pick out more of the same features of academic style.

Are not both psychology and sociology, then, it might be asked, equally concerned with the way individual behaviour is socially conditioned? The answer is 'Yes', but the psychologist's point of attention is usually the individual, the sociologist's that of the groups and categories to which the individual belongs. But that is to put it too crudely, for psychologists do study groups and categories, too: the attitudes, say, of miners, disc-jockeys, sadists, or women. The real difference is that the unit or frame of reference for the psychologist is the behaviour of the individual, whether his inner 'psyche' or its external manifestations observable in his relationships with others. The sociologist approaches perhaps exactly the same piece of behaviour 'from the other end', as it were, and asks what the significant regularities and patterns in a person's behaviour are that enable us to see him as typical of others who have been similarly socialized, undergone parallel life experiences, or belonged to similar groups. Social behaviour is thus not simply the putting together of all the separate 'natural' behaviours of many individuals—what is called 'aggregate psychology'—it is a qualitatively different *level* of behaviour, not 'given' in the *individual* psyche independently of its experience of society, as it were, but produced in *social groups* and internalized within the individual as a result of exposure to the pressures of these groups. Both the psychologist and the sociologist, then, may study the same behaviour and ask similar questions. It is not, crudely, that one studies the group and the other the individual, but that the focus or 'point of entry' will be the individual for the psychologist, and for the sociologist the society and culture of which the individual is a part. They will thus frequently converge in their studies, and at the borderlines it becomes rather arbitrary whether one labels a study 'psychology' or 'sociology'. Yet the psychologist, basically, is interested in the way the individual's behaviour is organised so as to constitute a 'personality', the sociologist in the way the individual as a person relates to others.

The differences between sociology and psychology, on the one hand then, are differences of *perspective*, in the same way as the differences between a sociologically minded historian and an 'empiricist' historian are differences of perspective. The differences between law, political science and economics, on the other hand, are differences of what one might term *domain*, in that each has a prime interest in certain substantive areas only within human behaviour in general, that is, the lawyer in the study of the way men resolve 'trouble issues', the economist in the study of production and consumption. Of course, at the widest, the lawyer who looks at the connection of law-making agencies to the rest of society, or who studies how different kinds of behaviour become defined as 'good' or 'bad' and how these definitions become embodied in law, is studying law in very sociological ways.

Researches within any one specific discipline may be vital to another: thus the sociologist may draw upon the economist's knowledge of the female labour-market as a part of his study of the family; conversely, the economist may use the sociologist's national surveys or local, intensive studies in order to enable him to estimate where and when likely supplies of labour, or demand for commodities, can be expected.

From P. Worsley (ed.) (1970), *Introducing Sociology*, 2nd edn Penguin, pp. 33–4.

Appendix

Writing a book review (see Chapter 10)

1 Here are two **examples** of instructions given by lecturers for book review assignments. Notice how the questions shape the structure that the review should take.

Book review in Political Economy (1500 words)

The review should not be a summary of the book. Instead it should state what the book sets out to do and assess how well the author achieves that goal. Your review might be *guided* by the following questions:

Objectives	What does the book set out to do?
Theory	Is there an explicit theoretical framework? If not, are there important theoretical assumptions?
Concepts	What are the central concepts? Are they clearly defined?
Argument	What is the central argument? Are there specific hypotheses?
Method	What methods are employed to test these?
Evidence	Is evidence provided? How adequate is it?
Values	Are value positions clear or are they implicit?
Literature	How does the work fit into the wider literature?
Contribution	How well does the work advance our knowledge of the subject?
Style	How clear is the author's language/style/expression?
Conclusion	What brief overall assessment is possible?

Book review in Women's Studies (1500 words)

I would like all students to produce a short critical book review . . . Some questions to ask yourself:

Who am I writing for?
What shared knowledge and values am I assuming?
Why does any of this matter?

Why should anyone believe me?
What are my reasons for thinking the way I do?
What is my evidence?

Formal qualities I shall look for include:

a evidence of understanding the book's basic terminology and
   argument;
b conceptual clarity;
c consistent and logical argument supported by evidence;
d independent judgement.

Content should include:

a a summary of the book's scope and argument;
b an assessment of the book in its own terms (i.e. how well does it do
   what it sets out to do?);
c an assessment of the book in your own terms (eg. is the topic
   worthwhile? does the book deal with the topic in the best way? how
   could it be improved?).

2 Here is a suggested **checklist** for the final draft of your book review.
Note that the questions in this checklist relate directly to the suggested
structure of the book review set out in Step 4 of *Writing the Review* in
Chapter 10.

1 Have I identified the book clearly, right at the start?
2 Is the author's argument clearly and objectively summarised so that
   my reader can recognise the theoretical approach and the range of
   material covered? (about a third of a short review)
3 Have I clearly identified and discussed the 2–3 key issues I wish to
   raise in relation to this book? (about 50% of the review)
4 Have I given reasons for my criticisms and my approval of different
   aspects of the book?
5 Is there a final evaluation of the book's importance, based on my
   previous discussion?

Appendix

Checklist for a psychology lab report (see Chapter 10)

Here is a detailed **checklist** for a psychology lab report made up by a lecturer for her first year class. It may give you some idea of the detailed expectations about the content, style and format of such a report.

1 **Title**
   Does it indicate:
   - topic area?
   - purpose of experiment?
   - direction of hypothesis?

2 **Abstract**
   necessary? length? full sentences? self-contained? does it cover each section of the report:
   - Intro (problem/hypothesis), i.e. purpose?
   - Methods (minimal relevant information), i.e. how experiment was done?
   - Results (significant data), i.e. findings?
   - Discussion (conclusions re hypothesis), i.e. implications?

3 **Introduction**
   Does it make clear:
   - topic of research interest:
       importance?
       definitions?
   - previous research findings:
       chronological?
       grouped by research focus/methodology?
       logical sequence in presentation?
   - gaps? weaknesses? area for extension?
       (leading to)
   - purpose of your experiment?
   - *does it state your hypothesis (or aim) clearly in final paragraph?*

(The Introduction section is presented in paragraphs, and previous research is briefly summarised rather than directly quoted. It should *persuade* your reader that your experiment has value and that your hypothesis is reasonable to explore.)

4 Method

Check:

- order of sub-headings?
- coverage of *all* information necessary for replication?
    only information necessary for replication?
- logical sequence of description of procedure?
- reference to Appendices for complex information?

(The Method section is always written in the past tense. The amount of detailed explanation of sample selection, design, apparatus, procedures, etc will depend on how relevant these factors are to your final discussion.)

5 Results

Tables, figures, etc:

- adequate title?
- units of measurement clearly indicated?
- statistical analysis identified?
- relevant findings only?

Text:

does it:

- direct attention to findings relevant to hypothesis?
- indicate relative importance of various findings?
- prepare reader for Discussion section to follow?
- refer to each table/figure in order?

is it:

- objective?
- self–contained?

(The Results section should be precise, succinct, crystal clear, and *not* evaluative.)

6 Discussion

Does it:

- *start by referring findings to hypothesis?*
- discuss individual findings in relation to research cited in Introduction?

If findings are unexpected/do not support hypothesis/conflict with previous research, does it indicate:

- possible sources of error:
    hypothesis?
    sample size/composition?
    materials?
    methods?
    classification of results?
- variations for subsequent experiments?

(The Discussion section is presented in paragraphs. It should direct your reader's attention to those aspects of the experiment which were successful in terms of your stated aim and hypothesis (and suggest the next step that might be taken), and those which were unsuccessful in terms of your hypothesis and previous research (and suggest variations in design, etc).)

7 **References:**
    correct format?
    all the sources referred to in report?
    only the sources referred to in report?
    absolutely accurate?

8 **Appendices:**
    clearly titled?
    raw data?
    complex methodology (questionnaires, scoring schedules, etc)?
    statistical analysis?

For **final editing** check:
    spelling, especially names, terms, capital letters
    grammatical sentences
    paragraph units
    headings/sub–headings
    references in text/final References
    tables, especially titles and numbers
    format requirements (cover sheet, margins, spacing, etc)

Appendix

Suggested reference books and supplementary materials (see Chapter 8)

General reference works

Longman Concise English Dictionary or *The Concise Oxford Dictionary* are the standard choices for a portable dictionary. For more intensive dictionary work, the two-volume *Shorter Oxford English Dictionary* is preferable, while in Australia *The Macquarie Dictionary* is also popular. For students whose first language is not English, the most comprehensive and clearly presented dictionary is A.S. Hornby's *Oxford Advanced Learner's Dictionary of Current English*.

Roget's Thesaurus is useful for helping you find the exact word.

The MLA Handbook (Modern Language Association of America, New York) is a standard reference manual for American and British academic writing.

Researching and writing essays, papers and theses

L. Blaxter, C. Hughes, and M. Tight (1996), *How to Research*, Open University Press, Buckingham UK.

P. Cryer (1996), *The Research Student's Guide to Success*, Open University Press, Buckingham UK.

L. Marshall and F. Rowland (1995), *A Guide to Learning Independently*, (2nd edn), Longman, Melbourne.

G. Taylor (1989), *The student's writing guide for the arts and social sciences*, CUP, Cambridge.

K.L. Turabian (1996), *A Manual for Writers of Term Papers, Theses and Dissertations*, (6th edn), University of Chicago Press, Chicago.

For science students wanting a comprehensive text on lab reports, articles and theses, the best current guide is:

D. Lindsay (1995), *A Guide to Scientific Writing*, (2nd edn), Longman, Melbourne.

English grammar, style and usage

J. Aitchison (1996), *Guide to Written English*, Cassell, London.

H.W. Fowler (1996) *The New Fowler's Modern English Usage*, (3rd edn: R.W. Burchfield), Oxford University Press, Oxford.

S. Greenbaum and J. Whitcut (1996), *Longman Guide to English Usage*, Penguin, London.

E. Partridge (1994), *Usage and Abusage*, (new edn: J. Whitcut), Penguin, London.

W. Strunk and E.B. White (1994), *Elements of Style*, (5th edn), Macmillan, New York.

A.J. Thomson and A.V. Martinet (1986), *A Practical English Grammar*, (4th edn), Oxford University Press, Oxford.

The best single hour's worth of reading on style probably remains George Orwell's famous essay 'Politics and the English Language', available in Orwell's volume *Inside the Whale and Other Essays* (Penguin) and in most collected editions of Orwell.

Aids to editing

The Guide to Australian Usage and Punctuation (1993), Collins Dove, Melbourne.

Style Manual for Authors, Editors and Printers (1994), 5 edn, AGPS, Canberra.

Internet and World Wide Web references

A. J. Kennedy (1996), *The Internet & World Wide Web: The Rough Guide 2.0*, Rough Guides Ltd., London.

Xia Li & N. Crane (1993), *Electronic Style: A Guide to Citing Electronic Information*, Meckler, Westport.

University of Chicago Press (1987), *Chicago Guide to Preparing Electronic Manuscripts: for Authors and Publishers*, Chicago.

Appendix

Direct quotations (see Chapter 8)

Whenever you use a direct quotation in an essay there are certain formalities which must be observed:

1 You must copy *exactly* the wording of the original text. If, for reasons of comprehension or grammatical coherence, additions or omissions are essential, then there are recognised procedures for handling this (see below).
2 Every direct quotation must be followed by a full *reference* to the source you took it from, including the precise page number(s) where the passage occurred. (See Appendix 14 for details of referencing styles.)
3 Any materials from which you quote must be included in your *bibliography.* (See Appendix 15 for details on bibliography.)

If these conventions are not observed in your essay, you may be accused of *plagiarism,* which is the academic sin of claiming the words and works of others as your own.

Format

When you include quotations in your essay, you should follow these general guidelines for format:

1 If the quotation takes up less than three lines in *your* hand-written or typed essay, then include it in the body of the essay and enclose it in quotation marks (either single or double).
2 If the quotation takes up *more than three lines,* then indent the whole quotation (that is, make the margins wider) and, if you are typing, use single-spacing. Quotation marks should *not* be used with this format.

Look at the following extract from a sociology essay and note the format used for the quotations:

If we examine the policy and practice of multiculturalism as it is emerging in Australia, it becomes obvious that although it is in part a response to ethnic pressures, it is much more a policy imposed by the dominant Anglo-Australian culture on the range of people inhabiting Australia. The ALP (1978:1) defines *ethnic* as 'all Australians and their children, whose mother tongue is not English'. It outlines:

> the ALP's avowed policy that Australia *is* a multi-cultural society in which all residents, regardless of ethnic origin and knowledge of English, should have equal rights and opportunities.   (ALP, 1978:2)

and continues:

> Within such a policy, there will be no more connotations of 'migrant' education, 'migrant' cultures, indeed of migrant problems, but rather of Australian education, of Australian culture, of Australian problems.
>
> (ALP, 1978:6)

Grassby, as Commissioner for Community Relations, points out, 'Australia *is* a "multi-cultural society" ' (1976:7) but admits that 'its institutions have not yet caught up with the reality' (1976:13). He argues for 'a full recognition of all the cultures and the languages. All must be equally cherished and nurtured within the context of the Australian family of the nation' (1976:13).

Special punctuation marks in direct quotations

1 When quoting a passage, if you *alter* or *add* anything to the exact words used by the original writer, you must indicate these changes by *square brackets*, thus [ ]. Such changes may be necessary in order to:
   - *add essential explanatory information*; for example, a passage from a history essay:

   In fine British tradition a peaceful co-existence was to be established at Botany Bay. The king stressed that

   > If any of our subjects shall wantonly destroy them [natives] . . . it is our will and pleasure that you cause such offenders to be brought to punishment according to the degree of offence. (10)

   From the outset all inhabitants of this continent were British subjects and, as such, equal before the law.

   - integrate the quotation into the *grammatical structure* of the essay; for example, a passage from a sociology essay:

MacKellar, in a recent policy statement made in his capacity as Minister for Immigration and Ethnic Affairs, makes some extraordinary distinctions between refugees

> with the sort of background, education and skills enabling them to fit readily into the Australian scene . . . (4)

and those

> who, it is assessed, would have extreme difficulty in adjusting to the Australian environment [and] who may not be best served by migration to Australia but [would] be better served by action by the UNHCR or other agencies to resettle them in a more compatible environment. (5)

- include a comment or indication of your own *opinion* about the material you are quoting, or to indicate an *error* (in which case you use the Latin 'sic', meaning 'thus', enclosed in square brackets). For example, a passage from a history essay:

> According to Senator Cristiano Otoni, speaking to the Brazilian Upper Chamber in 1883, before the end of the slave trade, owners had been 'careless as to the duration of the life [sic] of their slaves'.

Here the student uses [sic] to indicate a grammatical error—'life' instead of 'lives'—in the original text.

2 If you *leave out* words from a complete sentence in the original source, you indicate this omission by three dots, thus . . . Such omissions may be made:

- at the *beginning* or *end* of a passage, either in order to adjust the quotation to the grammar of your sentence or to omit less relevant material. However, if the quotation is clearly a syntactic fragment (only part of a longer sentence but clear in meaning in itself), then it is not essential to indicate omissions, especially at the beginning of the quotation. For example, a passage from an anthropology essay, where the omission of words from the direct quotation is not indicated as it occurs at the *start* of the original sentence:

> Literacy also 'equips people to perform the varied tasks required in the modernizing society' (Lerner, 1958: 60) and 'spreads the consumption of urban products beyond the city limits' (Lerner, 1958:61).

Here is a passage from a sociology essay where the omission of words from the quotation *is* indicated since it occurs at the *end* of the original sentence:

> Turning now to the sociological components of the study, it is firstly necessary to define what is sociological. 'Sociologists use the scientific method to learn how human groups are put together and how they function . . .' (Mack & Young, 1968:1).

• in the *centre* of a quotation, where certain phrases or clauses are not relevant to the point being made in your essay. In such cases the omission must *always* be indicated. For example, a passage from a prehistory essay:

> However, while it can be relatively easy to recognize patterns of behaviour and 'to infer from them some of the parameters of the activities which produced them, . . . it is much more difficult to determine the nature of the social unit which performed those activities' (Freeman, 1968, p. 265).

Appendix  14

References (see Chapter 8)

In an academic essay whenever you are

- quoting the exact words of another writer;
- closely summarising a passage from another writer;
- using an idea or material which is directly based on the work of another writer;

then you must identify and acknowledge your source in a systematic style of referencing. Otherwise you may be accused of *plagiarism* (see Appendix 13).

The three most common styles for references to printed and electronic materials are: footnotes, endnotes, and included references. Different departments within a university may favour different styles, so it is essential that you check on the preferred format for each course in which you are studying. Essays in literary criticism, for example, in which frequent reference is made to the same literary text, have their own characteristic style of citation.

In general, your aim must be to include in your reference all the information that is necessary for your reader to trace the source of your material easily and accurately.

Footnotes and endnotes

The first two systems of referencing, footnotes and endnotes, are very similar: in both you insert a number (either in brackets or slightly above the line) in your text at the end of a sentence or immediately following a direct quotation or a point taken from a source. For footnotes these numbers may either run consecutively through the whole essay or start afresh with (1) at the start of each new page; for endnotes the numbering is always consecutive. With footnotes the information about the source of each numbered reference is given at the bottom of each page of your text; with endnotes the same information is given in a consolidated list at the end of the essay.

Format: The following points should be noted, both for use in your own essays and to enable you to interpret the footnotes and endnotes you encounter in your reading:

1 On a *first citation* of a work, full details, as in the bibliography, must be given, together with a *precise page reference*, for example, 'R. Beard (1970), *Teaching and Learning in Higher Education*, Penguin, London, p. 49.'

2 *Subsequent references* to the same work may be cited by:
 • short form: the writer's name, the short title, and the page number, e.g. Beard, *Teaching and Learning*, pp. 89–91.
 • op. cit.: (i.e. *opere citato*, Latin, 'in the work cited') This is used following the writer's name and followed by the page reference when the citation is to the same work referred to earlier but not in the immediately preceding footnote. It may or may not be underlined.
  e.g. 1 M. Douglas (1973), *Natural Symbols*, Penguin, London, p. 88.
   2 R. Fox (1967), *Kinship and Marriage*, Penguin, London, p. 161.
   3 M. Douglas, op. cit., p. 132.

 • ibid.: (i.e. *ibidem*, Latin, 'in the same place') This is used, with a following page number, when the citation is to the same work referred to in the immediately preceding footnote. It may or may not be underlined,
  e.g. 1 M. Douglas (1973), *Natural Symbols*, Penguin, London, p. 68
   2 ibid., pp. 70–71
   3 ibid., p. 173

3 *Other common abbreviations* in references:
 • loc. cit. (*loco citato*, 'in the place already quoted') has confused usage (and you would probably be wise to avoid it in your own writing). It is sometimes used in place of op. cit. when the reference is to an article or chapter rather than a book. It is sometimes used in place of ibid. when the citation is to the same source and the same page as the immediately preceding reference. It is sometimes used in place of op. cit. when the citation is to the same page as the previous citation to the same source.
 • f. (or ff.) ('and the following page(s)') is used to indicate frequent references to an item within a few consecutive pages, e.g. R. Fox, *Kinship and Marriage*, p. 71f.

- <u>passim</u> ('scatteredly') is used when the reference is to items to be found throughout that source or that section of a book, e.g. Beard, *Teaching and Learning*, <u>passim</u>.

4 *Complex references.* If you are citing a quotation or material which you have found already quoted by another writer, include in your citation both the full bibliographic details of the original quotation (which you will find in the reference) and the details of the book in which you found it, e.g. H. Cox (1968), *The Secular City*, Penguin, London, p. 93, quoted in M. Douglas (1973), *Natural Symbols*, Penguin, London, p. 37.

Included references

In this third style of referencing, which is commonly used in science and the social sciences, all references are cited in the body of your text. The references are extremely brief (writer's name, date of publication, page number) and the full bibliographic information is supplied in the bibliography. Some styles of included referencing use p. or pp. to indicate page numbers. Others use a colon : between the year and the page number.

Format:

1 If the writer's name appears in the text of your essay, the remaining items of the citation will follow this in brackets,

> e.g. Beard (1970: pp. 91–92) argues that concept learning is important.

(Here the actual argument is found on pages 91 and 92.)

> e.g. Fox (1967) demonstrates the close relationship between kinship and marriage in certain societies.

(As this relationship is the theme of the whole book, no specific page references are given.)

2 If the writer's name does not appear in the text of your essay, the reference must include his or her name within the brackets and should come at the end of a sentence or immediately following a direct quotation,

> e.g. It has been argued that concept learning is important (Beard, 1970, pp. 91–92).

Comparison of referencing styles

Each style of referencing has characteristic advantages:

1 **Footnotes** make it easy for the reader to identify a source immediately merely by glancing to the bottom of the page. However, lengthy footnotes, including comments and additional information, can be distracting and clumsy.
2 **Endnotes** permit extended commentary and additional information, but require the reader to refer constantly between the actual text and the final pages of the essay.
3 **Included references** are extremely efficient but can only identify a source and allow no room for additional comments.

In order to demonstrate these styles of referencing more clearly, we have taken a passage from a student's prehistory essay and used included references in version 1 and footnotes in version 2. Endnotes represent the version 2 style, except that the citations for the whole essay would be listed at the end.

Version 1
The work of van Lawick-Goodall (1971), Kortlandt and van Zon (1968), and Wright (1972) shows that present-day chimpanzees, orangutans and macaque monkeys are capable of using simple tools and bipedal locomotion. Wright (1972, p. 305) concluded, after tool-using experiments with a captive orangutan, that manipulative disability is not a factor which would have prevented Australopithecines from mastering the fundamentals of tool technology. However, while there is an unquestionable validity in comparing the behaviour of present-day apes with early hominids, it is important to note, as Howells (1973, p. 53) says, 'a Pantroglodyte is not and cannot be the ancestor of man. He cannot be an ancestor of anything but future chimpanzees.'

However, van Lawick–Goodall (1971, p. 233) suggests that the modern chimpanzee shows a type of intelligence closer to that of man than is found in any other present-day mammal. She argues that

> . . . the chimpanzee is, nevertheless, a creature of immense significance to the understanding of man . . . He has the ability to solve quite complex problems, he can use and make tools for a variety of purposes . . . Who knows what the chimpanzees will be like forty million years hence? (van Lawick-Goodall, 1971, pp. 244–245)

The bibliography following the essay from which this passage was taken includes the following items:

Howells, W. (1973), *Evolution of the Genus Homo*, Addison–Wesley Pub. Co.
Kortlandt, A. & van Zon, J.C.J. (1968), 'The present state of research on the dehumanization hypothesis of African ape evolution', *Proc. 2nd Int. Congr. Primatol.*, Atlanta, pp. 10–13.
van Lawick–Goodall, J. (1971), *In the Shadow of Man*, Collins.
Wright, R.V.S. (1972), 'Imitative learning of a flaked-stone technology', *Mankind* 8, pp. 296–306.

Version 2

The work of van Lawick-Goodall,[1] Kortlandt and van Zon,[2] and Wright[3] shows that present-day chimpanzees, orangutans and macaque monkeys are capable of using simple tools and bipedal locomotion. Wright concluded, after tool-using experiments with a captive orangutan, that manipulative disability is not a factor which would have prevented Australopithecines from mastering the fundamentals of tool technology.[4] However, while there is unquestionable validity in comparing the behaviour of present-day apes with early hominids, it is important to note, as Howells says, 'a Pantroglodyte is not and cannot be the ancestor of man. He cannot be an ancestor of anything but future chimpanzees.'[5]

However, van Lawick-Goodall suggests that the modern chimpanzee shows a type of intelligence closer to that of man than is found in any other present-day mammal.[6] She argues that

> . . . the chimpanzee is, nevertheless, a creature of immense significance to the understanding of man . . . He has the ability to solve quite complex problems, he can use and make tools for a variety of purposes. . . Who knows what the chimpanzees will be like forty million years hence?[7]

---

1. J. van Lawick-Goodall (1971), *In the Shadow of Man*, Collins.
2. A. Kortlandt & J.C.J. van Zon (1968), 'The present state of research on the dehumanization hypothesis of African ape evolution', *Proc. 2nd Int. Congr. Primatol*, Atlanta, pp. 10–13
3. R.V.S. Wright (1972), 'Imitative learning of a flaked-stone technology', *Mankind* 8, pp. 296–306
4. ibid., p. 305.
5. Howells (1973), *Evolution of the Genus Homo*, Addison–Wesley Pub. Co., p. 53
6. van Lawick-Goodall, op. cit., p. 233
7. ibid., pp. 244–245

References to Internet sources

Systems for referencing material taken from Internet sources are still evolving, and you will find a variety of conventions in use. In principle—whether you are using a system of included references, footnotes or endnotes—try to follow the same basic pattern as we have set out above.

For included references (the Harvard system), this should present few problems. You will simply give the author's name (or organisation's title) and the date of publication at the appropriate point in your sentence—except that with electronic sources you should give the month and even day of publication as well as the year if these details are available,

e.g. Smith (6 April, 1997) argues . . .

If your source is not a published one on a Web site but, say, a personal communication via e-mail, then indicate this,

e.g. Smith (private e-mail message, 6 April, 1997) argues . . .

If the Web page or site you want to reference does not have a date of publication, indicate this by the use of 'n.d.' (not dated) in the place where you would normally supply the date.

For footnotes and endnotes, the principles set out earlier in this Appendix apply, except that for the *name of the publisher* you will normally give the *title of the Web host site*, and for the *place of publication* you will supply the *Internet address of the site*. For a worked example of this—and for an example of how to set out full details for an e-mail citation—see Section E in the appendix which follows (*Appendix 15: Bibliography*).

Appendix  15

Bibliography (see Chapter 8)

Following every academic written assignment you are required to give a bibliography. This is an alphabetical list of all the printed and electronic sources of material you have found useful while preparing to write the assignment.

The ordering of items and the format of your bibliography are important. The style required may vary slightly from one discipline to another, *so always check if there are any specific departmental instructions about the format which you must observe.* Otherwise you can follow the pattern of bibliography used in any textbook for the course.

Here is an example of a bibliography which observes common practice. It is followed by a commentary on the points to be noted in the format.

Bibliography

Australian Dictionary of Biography, vol. 6, 1976, 'Trugernanner'.

Australian Law Reform Commission (1986), *Aboriginal Customary Law*, AGPS, Canberra.

Bird, G. (1988), *The Process of Law in Australia: Intercultural Perspectives*, Butterworths, Sydney.

Bourke C. & H. Cox (1994), 'Two Laws: One Land', in (eds) C. Bourke, E. Bourke & B. Edwards, *Aboriginal Australia*, Univ. of Queensland Press, St Lucia.

The Canberra Times (1997), 'Hysteria on native title case', January 5, p.6.

Dodson, P. (1989), 'Statehood for Northern Territory', *Aboriginal Law Bulletin*, vol. 2, no. 39, pp. 14–16.

——(1993), 'Reconciliation and the High Court's decision on native title', *Aboriginal Law Bulletin*, vol. 3, no. 61, pp. 6–9.

Hanks, J. (1991), *Constitutional Law in Australia*, Butterworths, Sydney.

Howard, C. (1993), 'The Mabo case', *Adelaide Review*, February, pp. 8–9.

Reynolds, H. (April 1996), 'After Mabo, What About Aboriginal Sovereignty?', *australian humanities review* [http://www.lib.latrobe.edu.au/AHR/archive/Issue-April 1996/Reynolds.html], acc. 6 March, 1997.

Points to notice:

A Organisation of list

1 All books, articles and other sources are listed in *alphabetical order* by surname of writer (or organisation producing the source, see first two items in the above bibliography for examples). If more than one book or article is listed for the same writer (see Dodson example), they are arranged by date of publication. If they are both published in the same year, refer to them as 1989a and 1989b.

The alphabetical arrangement is a clear method of organising material and corresponds with the organisation of card and on-line catalogues and the arrangement of books, within sections, on the library shelves.

2 Some departments require you to make *separate lists* for books and for articles and government documents, or for primary and secondary sources.

B Books

1 The author's *surname* is followed by initials or first name (see Bird example).

If you are referring to a chapter by a particular writer which is included in a larger book, list the chapter under the writer's name and follow this with the full details of the editor's name, book title, etc. (see Bourke and Cox).

2 The *date* of publication must be included, either as the final item in the reference, or immediately following the writer's name as in this bibliography.

3 The *title* of the book is italicised, bolded or underlined (see Bird). (This is what you look for as you run your eye along the library shelf.)

4 The title is followed by the *name of the publisher* and the *place/city of publication*. Some departments require only one or the other item. Be consistent in the pattern you follow and in the punctuation you use (see Bird). (This information can be useful in establishing whether the book is written for an American or Australian audience.)

C Articles

1 The *title* of the article or chapter is enclosed by quotation marks and followed by a comma. (Note: It is *not* italicised, bolded or underlined like the title of a book or journal. In other words, depending on whether you used italics, bold or underlining to indicate book titles (B3 above), you use a different format for the title of the article or chapter.)

2 The *name of the journal* is italicised, bolded or underlined in the same format you use for book titles. (This is what you look for on the library shelf.)

3 Full details of the journal are given, including (where relevant) the volume number, series number, date of issue, and the page references for the article being cited (see Dodson).

D Government publications, newspapers, reference books, reports, etc.

1 Official publications are usually listed with the department or institution as the writer (see Australian Law Reform Commission).

2 Standard reference books, such as encyclopaedias, are listed by their titles (see *Australian Dictionary of Biography*).

3 Newspaper items which are not signed are listed by the name of the newspaper (see *The Canberra Times*).

E Internet sources

Wherever possible, follow the basic principles as listed for books and articles above.

1 The author's *surname*, followed by initials or first name (see Reynolds example for this and each of the points that follow).

2 *Date of publication*, including the day and month as well as year, if available and appropriate.

3 *Title of the document* (or the *Web page*) in quotation marks.

4 *Title of the Complete Work* or the *Web host site* in which the specific document resides, normally italicised.

5 *Internet address*, in square brackets. Take care here to be accurate, especially if the address is long. Wherever possible, copy the address directly from the Web site details using the Copy function on your Edit menu rather than trusting your hand and eye to get it right!

6 *Date* at which you accessed the document (visited the site). This is important because of the speed with which information and sites on the Web appear, and then often change or even disappear altogether. Date of access is distinguished from date of publication by its placement (at the end of the bibliographic item) and by the use of an abbreviated signal such as 'acc.' for accessed.

If you wish to cite a private, interactive (as distinct from published) source such as a personal comment received via e-mail, one system commonly in use is:

author of email. [author's e-mail address]. "Broad subject of message". Status of message and name of addressee, [addressee's e-mail address]. Date.

For example, a reply by one of the authors of this book to an e-mail enquiry from a student about how to cite e-mail sources, would be cited thus:

Clanchy, John. [John.Clanchy@anu.edu.au]. "Citing e-mail sources". Private e-mail message to Cheryl Student, [Cheryl.Student@anu.edu.au]. 6 August 1997.

Conventions for electronic citation and bibliographic format are still much more fluid than those for printed sources. The safest route for the moment is to follow a system that mimics as closely as possible that for printed documents. Remember, the purpose of providing a bibliography of your sources is so that your reader can follow in your tracks—and for that he or she will need: author's name, date of publication, title of the document (or Web page), an Internet address where it can be found, and the date of access. (For much more detailed accounts of electronic citation and bibliographic referencing—including such sources as e-mail communications and Usenet discussion groups—see the texts listed in *Appendix 12.*)

F Annotated bibliographies

Some departments require you to produce annotated bibliographies, that is, with a brief comment following each item which both summarises the scope of the book or article and indicates in what way it was of particular significance to your purposes in writing your essay.

Hart, C.M.W. and Pilling, A.R. (1960), *The Tiwi of North Australia*, Holt, Rinehart & Winston, New York.

This is the standard monograph on the Tiwi comprising the earlier work of Hart on the ceremonies, social organisation, economic system and daily life of this Aboriginal people, and the more recent description of the Tiwi in the 1960s by Pilling. It was particularly useful in providing an insight into the various forms of social control which operate in an island community.

Note: It is essential to head all the notes you take from printed materials with the full bibliographic information you might need if you later want to use material from the book or article in an essay or refer to the source in your own bibliography. Also remember to include page references for any major ideas or key quotations you include in your notes.